Partly is a wonderland greenhouse that Jack built and then allowed us to enter and it glows like a signal that means human beings can be great observers and creators of beauty and fun, all because of what exists. Greatest are the computer anagrams and statements that lay out some lovely mistakes.

BERNADETTE MAYER, AUTHOR OF *WORKS AND DAYS*

Jack Collom and his poetry were inseparable. Both were humorously profound, and right up to the end filled with an (almost) innocent wonder at all the world has to offer. Language was his toy, his place, his way of communicating with us and with nature.

LUCY R. LIPPARD, AUTHOR OF *UNDERMINING: A WILD RIDE THROUGH LAND USE, POLITICS AND ART IN THE CHANGING WEST*

Jack Collom lived a life of poetry as few ever do or could—not just sharp and freshly-moving poems, but a heart of compassion and quiet jest; constant open eye and spirit for the youngest and oldest beings who crossed his path. Jack was the very meaning of "soul." His legacy is more than just writings and teachings, it's a whole life. It will grow.

GARY SNYDER, AUTHOR OF *THE GREAT CLOD: NOTES AND MEMORIES ON THE NATURAL HISTORY OF CHINA AND JAPAN*

I0370594

Jack Collom wrote with a wider range and bigger heart than any other North American poet of the past 100 years. His books are field guides to everything that makes you love poetry. *Partly* is like a great day's scramble through bramble bushes, bogs, over boulders, under trees, into the world of birds, vernacular speech, posters of snow leopards, moss, lichen, watch out for that cactus! It is fun and rough & tumble. I'd rather spend a day with a Jack Collom book than in the Library of Congress.

ANDREW SCHELLING, AUTHOR OF *TRACKS ALONG THE LEFT COAST: JAIME DE ANGULO AND PACIFIC COAST CULTURE*

Jack Collom's poetic ethos is resoundingly affirmative. In a word? Everything. In poetry, Collom found a resource that couldn't be extinguished—"made of meaning and unmeaning," and seeded with "embryo specks of beauty and kindness." No harmony, no dissonance, no particular, no universal, no absurdity nor tenderness need be—could ever be!—excluded from his exploration. (As he writes in the reface to this book, "Noticed I was discovering (not simply recording) what I knew.") To read these poems is to understand that poetry is breath which becomes the lung, breathing through and with it. How fortunate that we can respire and inspire with Jack Collom, for here is a poet who had the humility to know that absolutely nothing was beneath his attention and the genius to track poetry's wonder into endlessness.

ELIZABETH ROBINSON, AUTHOR OF *ON GHOSTS AND RUMOR*

Partly is a mischievously dizzying Selected, a taste of a treasured legacy that eco-poet and master writing teacher Jack Collom edited before he died. We have in hand rambling, gritty, soaring instances of his practices: calligrammes, acrostics, anagrams, drawings, collaborations with students and friends, and perky sonnets with ear to Shakespeare. Collom always had an infectious metabolism with poetry; it was vibratory in him and words rose naturally, nothing too precious or elevated for the construct at hand. He was in the lineage of WC Williams and Gertrude Stein and the innovators of the New American Poetry and a major poet of the community of the Jack Kerouac School at Naropa where he famously taught and made one think and write and care about the world: its words, its kinetics of the human and other remarkable celestial and earthy kin for many years. Here's mud in the eye! "The angle doesn't matter,/Turn & stagger upward, mad as a hatter."

ANNE WALDMAN, AUTHOR OF *TRICKSTER FEMINISM*

Partly, Jack Collom's last personally selected poems written over many decades, is a rambling trove of his left-hand poetics of the ordinary and the fanciful, the quick and the careful. If ordinary and fanciful, care and quickness seem contradictory, they are not in these poems (and graphics) where they are made and arrive in the same gesture. This is what I have always loved in Jack's poetry, the warmth of personal feeling in the spontaneous take and movability of context allowed for the words chosen, or lines drawn. Little concern for direction and finish-line, these poems are made from his momentary love of this act.

REED BYE, AUTHOR OF *JOIN THE PLANETS*

In Jack Collom's final manuscript, *Partly*, we see the early and last fruits of a great poet who uses the page as a canvas to explore and invent the open field of language. For Collom, "Poetry is the nervous system's nervous system," a felicitous marriage of brain and body. His project remains true to the enactment of experimentation for many decades, formal in the best sense, a poet who plays with and constructs every imaginable form—often embedding handmade images and color to collage a single word—ekphrastic, elastic, acrostic, calligramatic. Seriously goofy and erudite, Collom's work is a poetic treasure hunt to a place and notion called Paradox where "there's a tiny gap/that leads to Paradise." And in this paradise, Jack Collom's poetry is a divine witness to place, bird, animal, and the entire natural world.

GLORIA FRYM, AUTHOR OF *THE TRUE PATRIOT*

Spanning from 1954 to close to now, this final manuscript is yet just a tantalizing taste of Jack Collom's astonishingly and magnificently various lifetime oeuvre. Few equal Jack's passionate investigation of form, from sonnets to acrostics to concrete poems to new forms invented uniquely for whatever he was discovering that moment. Each poem seems to insist that the reader be included in its writing, and collaborations especially point to Jack's inclusiveness—of the people around him, of all vocabulary, of nature's unknown wildness, of the pigeons as well as the warblers. May his expansive spirit continue to inspire us!

MARCELLA DURAND, AUTHOR OF *RAYS OF THE SHADOW*

Jack Collom's work is one of the most diverse poetic geographies on the planet. In *Partly*, you will find poems acrostic, aphoristic, asemic, abecedarian, bold, collaborative, concrete, calligraphic, disruptive, delightful, ecological, evolutionary, formal, fantastic, generous, glyphic, humorous, innovative, joyful, Kharm-ic, lyric, morphing, nonsensical, ornithological, paradoxical, quotidian, relational, sonic, technical, typographic, unpretentious, visual, wondrous, Xeroxed, yarn-ful, and zoological. All that and more – and "a sad, sad star-chicken" too!

E.J. MCADAMS, AUTHOR OF *TRANSECTs*

Jack Collom realized that it's a Long Long Sacred Haul, from what they call juvenilia to the full blown lines of a poet's "acme," and then the Final Flow. He was indeed on a Sacred Trail. His good will, his profound sense of humor, and his utmost concern for the apt Survival of Humankind and all Plants and Animals, shine forth in his work. Jack's worth slowing down for, and worth the expending of daily study and pondering. In his remarkable history traced in his poetry, he lives on and on and on.

ED SANDERS, AUTHOR OF *BROKEN GLORY: THE FINAL YEARS OF ROBERT F. KENNEDY*

Jack Collom was a great inventor, whose goal was to destabilize the world of poetry, and cut through all the repressive forces to make something fresh, instantly renewable, and true to life. Every poem was like a new morning, a fresh take, as if seen through the eyes of a child, as if a measure of caprice was the magic light which gives life meaning. His total work is intrepid, incorrigible, and spills over the side of the page, with an endless rigor, an intelligence, and an intuitive sense of when to stop and go on. All the splendor in the grass is right here.

LEWIS WARSH, AUTHOR OF *OUT OF THE QUESTION*

Toward the end of the short prefatory comment that Jack Collom wrote for this collection, he wrote, "Variety is the basic fact." Certainly, as the works that comprise *Partly* make clear, this remark speaks directly to Jack's poetry: formal variety, thematic variety, variations on the iamb or other ruling metric unit, and sometimes elements so various on a page as to push plenitude toward gorgeous messiness: the rush of ungovernable life. And, ultimately, it is of life that the observation "Variety is the basic fact" speaks. No poet ever has been so delighted by life and generous in the living of his own. *Partly* is Jack Collom's parting gift to life, a work of sheer affirmation carried out over a lifetime of intellectual and linguistic vivacity. It is a masterpiece of happiness, ever seriously but mischievously at play with happenstance. Thank you, Jack.

LYN HEJINIAN, AUTHOR OF *THE BOOK OF A THOUSAND EYES*

When Jack was alive, he was my favorite living poet—although I was unable really to separate my love of his work from my love of him. Now that he's died, he joins my personal pantheon, including the usual suspects and Jubilee saints. Do they yodel in Heaven?

Peter Lamborn Wilson, author of *Black Fez Manifesto*

And Jack, Jack wrote on his hand every day,
in ballpoint: numbers, titles, words
of high note as we walked, all that way

with sunflowers in it, swallows
up and out one by one to cloverleaf
and stamp the very fact of flight,

the emerald polar-green it's always been
in glints and shimmers, now the rose-rare violet—
eyes fly it like a kite.

Merrill Gilfillan, author of *Would-be Dogwood*

Collom's work avoids the Romantic "pitfall" of reifying the division between nature and the intellect, by bringing together unlikely tonal combinations, particularly the playful and the serious.

Cole Heinowitz, author of "Letter to Olson"

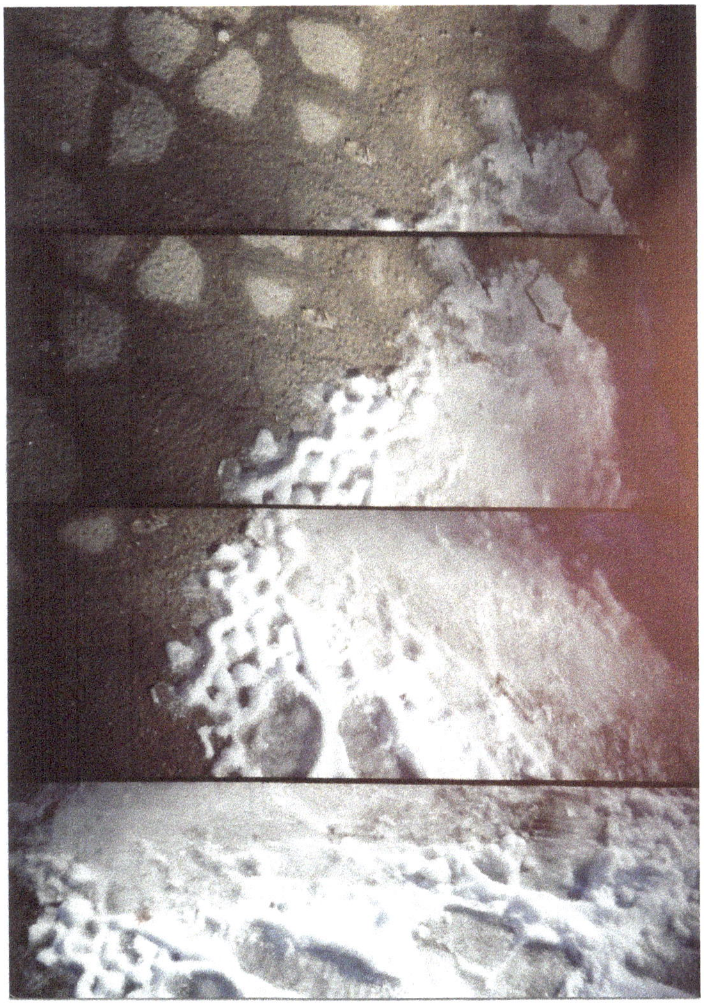

PARTLY

SELECTED POEMS: 1954-2016

JACK COLLOM

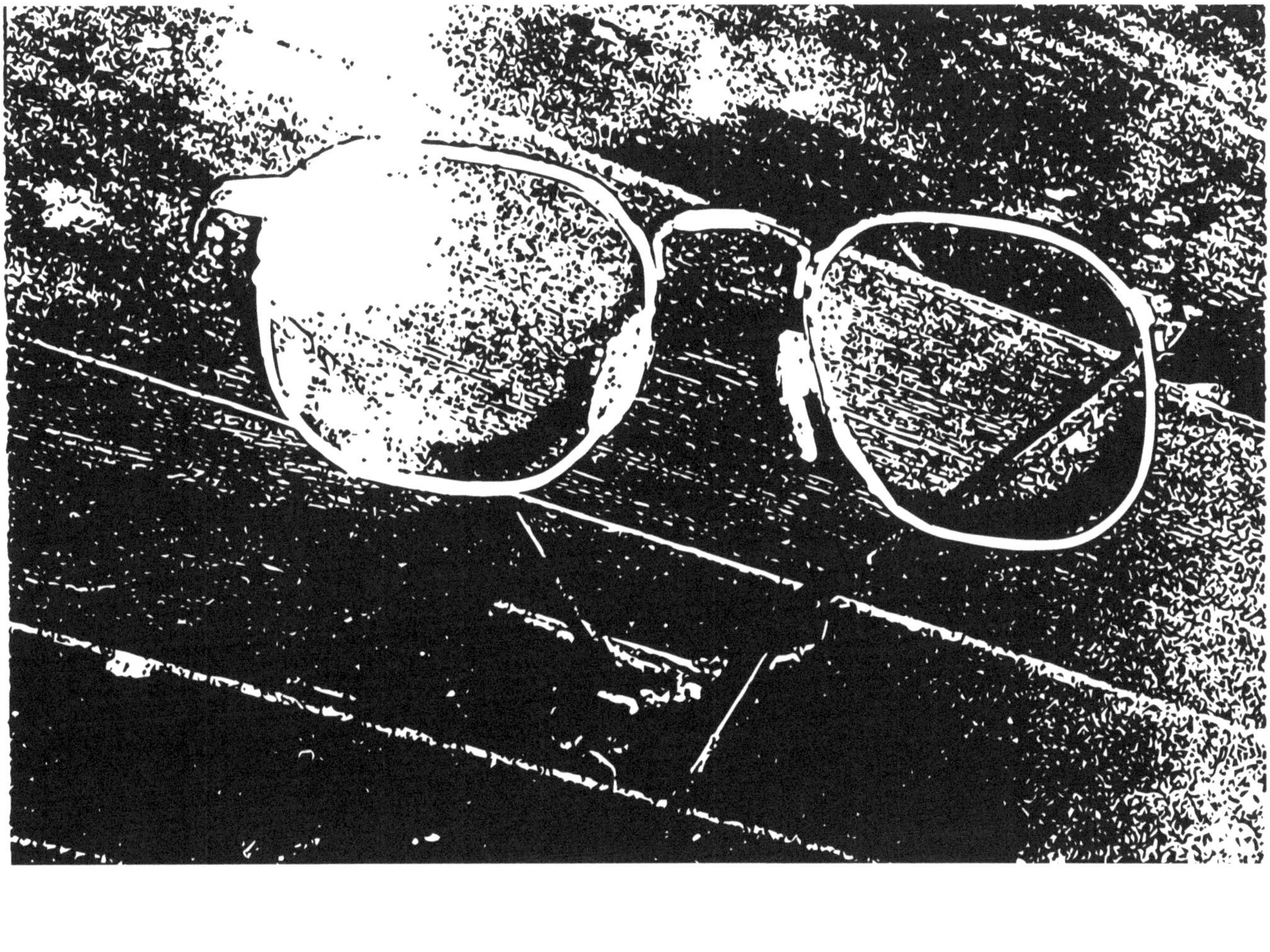

Spuyten Duyvil
New York City

The following poems have been previously published:

"Why I Was Late for Work" (*The Task*, Baksun Books, 1996)

"Equals" (*Entering the City*, The Backwaters Press, 1997)

("We Have Bulk Soap"), ("Avant-garde Final"), ("WOKE up this morning") and "Local names poems for Mom at Jane's" (*Dog Sonnets*, Jensen-Daniels, 1998)

In his last year, Jack Collom searched through his many manila envelopes of poems written over the course of this life, most of which had never been published, except in his own self-published and illustrated chapbooks, circulated among friends and colleagues. The publication of *Partly* fulfills Collom's great wish that this selection of unpublished works would comprise a final book.

ISBN 978-1-947980-45-7 pbk. ISBN 978-1-947980-54-9 hdc.

Library of Congress Cataloging-in-Publication Data

Names: Collom, Jack, 1931- 2017.
Title: Partly / Jack Collom.
Description: New York : Spuyten Duyvil, [2018]
Identifiers: LCCN 2018006776 | ISBN 9781947980457
Classification: LCC PS3553.O47633 A6 2018 | DDC 811/.54--dc23
LC record available at https://lccn.loc.gov/2018006776

CONTENTS

INTRODUCTION

In Stefan Hyner's wonderful 2017 chapbook, *An Even Older Memory*, dedicated to Jack, he notes, "Charles Olson insisted that poetry was a twenty-four-hour job with no break, no golden years of retirement, and a very badly paid one on top of it, cuz no government in its 'right' mind would provide for people whose sole purpose rests with the destruction of that government."

Jack Collom, of course, was an Olson devotee, and reading this, I realized that it was precisely the way he lived (me tagging along for more than three decades, occasionally befuddled). He wrote constantly, cared little for material things, taught adults and children with supreme skill and enthusiasm, was relentlessly curious and sidesplittingly funny, gave no thought to Babbitty pensions and security, produced work that skewered the State, consistently lambasted capitalism and especially attacked those forces destroying the Earth. Nature was his best friend.

Jack was a lifelong active environmentalist and a lifelong avid birdwatcher. As he lay dying, his son Chris and I put on a CD of bird calls (we'd also played Robert Johnson, Yodelin' Slim Clark, Blind Willie Johnson and other musicians Jack loved). Jack was fading and I was dozing next to him, struggling not to fall asleep to the lullabies of warblers and meadowlarks. At 2:45 AM, a loon shrieked and wailed, a loud, eerie quaver that startled me bolt upright. I rushed to the other side of the bed in time to be with Jack for his last breath. Turns out, he was right: birds are reliable messengers—"exchanges of earth and sky."

Earlier that day, a hospice nurse came to check on Jack. She let us know that he'd "transitioned" and would soon be gone. I mentioned his flailing arms—as if he were dancing (and sometimes I danced with him). She told me it's a syndrome called "terminal agitation." Then she added confidently that Jack was seeking and trying to embrace the loved ones who'd gone before and were waiting above, in heaven. I scowled at her, maybe even sneered, but said nothing. Instead I thought, "Stand back, lady! This man is a poet. He's not grasping for heaven, he's reaching for the right word!"

Jack Collom spent his life reaching for the right words.

Jennifer Heath
Boulder, Colorado
2018

Foreword
Margaret Ronda

Partly: as in a component piece, one means of approach among many, an attention to a particular amidst a larger whole. Holding together division and relation, the term opens space for different perspectives to coexist, irreducibly. It conveys a process of thinking as it unfolds, phoneme by phoneme, perception by perception. At the same time, *partly* can suggest an attention to other scales of thought, pointing to something previously overlooked or what is not yet known. "Poetry," Jack Collom writes, "is made of meaning / as well as unmeaning." In Collom's marvelously various work gathered in this volume, this sense of the partial emerges as the creative condition of possibility governing each poetic utterance, a generativity that ceaselessly opens toward new ideas, new forms.

Partly—adverb and book—illuminates Collom's lifelong poetic practice as a commitment to the aspectual, the multivalent, the contradictory, the generative. Across his voluminous body of work, Collom's writing enacts a dynamic play of processual thinking, a *going by parts*. In his astonishingly active poems, Collom registers the restless energy of consciousness as it unfolds in sound and syntax, pattern and parataxis. As he writes in one poem from this volume, "dualistic series on the coming oneness":

> I'd like being nothing but clear
> but have to say
>   what truer here to me
> less clear more
> it seems
> unsettled

Or as he writes wryly in another poem, "Why are my thoughts so motherfucking goosey?" This playful, deft attention to the essential "goosiness" of poetic thinking, its unsettled and variable motion, is on display in this collection of previously unpublished poetry.

Gathering material spanning Collom's life, from early pieces in the 1950s and 1960s through poems written shortly before his death in July 2017, *Partly* provides a vantage into the remarkable diversity and inventive range of Collom's work. From acrostics to concrete poems, found poems to abecedarians, recipes and sonnets to descriptions of dreams, these writings take poetry in all directions. Alive to the shapeliness and surprise of language unfolding in time, Collom's compositions refuse categorical distinctions that would separate out the formal from the improvisational, the serious from the humorous, the philosophical from the bawdy. These works evoke, instead, the varieties of experience arising in a given moment and the exactitude of insight poetry can bring to bear on these experiences. While many of these poems offer explicit meditations on the work of poetry, the book as a whole elaborates an *ars poetica*, an extended reflection on what he calls poetry's motivating "tensions between surprise / and the expected."

For Collom, poetry is an artistic mode that uniquely embodies, via the constraints of form, a dialectical play of expectation and novelty, order and complexity. Far from being static or rote, poetry's formal designs become an ever-various way of organizing the energies of language, giving lived experience a knowable shape. Poetic form in Collom's writing foregrounds the forms of being and living that structure our lives, thus enabling us to see them anew. At the same time, form frequently emerges as the locus of ludic high-jinks across Collom's work. Collom everywhere insists on pleasure and good humor as a necessary stance toward the world, even when his work takes on weighty themes. Humor, particularly as evoked in and through poetic forms—the dirty limerick ("Lime Rickeys") or scatological acrostic—reminds the reader of the essential pleasure in poetry, its connection with childhood play, and the gleeful delight to be found in the ribald joke.

Here, every thing, every instance of thought and momentary experience, becomes fodder for poetry. In this sense, Collom's everyday *poiesis* can be traced back to the American modernism of William Carlos Williams, with his emphasis on ordinary objects, colloquial language, and immediate sensory perception. Like Williams, Collom develops an idiom that is often deceptively casual in its evocation of the vibrant parts and patterns that characterize a daily surround (Williams' Paterson, Collom's Boulder). Collom's frequent use of short lines and his insistence on clarity and fresh insight bears further connections to Williams' innovations. Collom's most direct homage to Williams can be found in his concrete poem from this collection, "Bill Was Right." Here, Collom puts extended pressure on Williams' most well-known phrase, from *Paterson*:

No ideas but in things.	NO
Ideas but in things. No	IDEAS
But in things. No ideas	BUT
In things. No ideas but	IN
Things. No ideas but in	THINGS.
No ideas but in things.	NO
Ideas but in things. No	IDEAS
But in things. No ideas	BUT
In things. No ideas but	IN
Things. No ideas but in	THINGS.
No ideas but in things.	NO
ideas but in things. No	IDEAS

But in things. No ideas	BUT
In things. No ideas but	IN

In Collom's hands, this phrase becomes koan-like, a meditative object. With each recalibration, Collom draws intensified attention to the thingliness of each word—the *fullness* of its *part*—but also to the balance of the phrase, its structural integrity and heft. Ending not with the noun ("things") but the preposition ("IN"), however, Collom shifts orientation away from things and toward a more ongoing energy of motion, relation, and immersion. Excavating new insight from Williams' phrase, Collom claims original ground for his own poetic practice (in characteristically understated way).

Situating Collom's poetry within a Williamsian tradition of American poetics that discovers in quotidian life a limitless trove of materials for experiment, we can draw links between his work and various avant-garde poetic movements of the postwar period: New York School, Language poetry, Black Mountain, Beat/Naropa. Such connections position Collom's work firmly within the broader lineages of the New American Poetry, while also underscoring his fundamental poetic originality and distinctiveness, his movement-of-one "poeting about," as he puts it. In its cataloging of the momentary happening in its varied intensities, Collom's writing resonates with the work of New York School poets such as Frank O'Hara, John Ashbery, and James Schuyler, and is even more closely aligned with second-generation figures such as Bernadette Mayer. While both Collom and Mayer draw on the witty observations and all-inclusive cultural registers of these first-generation New York School writers, they take these approaches into new experiential terrain, whether domestic or ecological. At the same time, they foreground the complexities of linguistic play to a greater and more various degree than their immediate New York School predecessors. In this regard, Collom's poetry, like Mayer's, can also be associated with the practices of Language poetry, with its exploration of the structuring frameworks and ideological codes of language.

Collom's engagement with the techniques and ideas motivating Language poetry is most clearly visible in his emphasis on the poem as a site of inquiry into language itself, its structures, flows, and logics. This approach emerges through Collom's emphasis on juxtaposition, his metonymic associations, and his ironizing invocations of the commodified language of advertising and political discourse. In one poem culled from the pages of the (now-defunct) *Rocky Mountain News,* Collom draws fragments from various news stories together to create what Lyn Hejinian would call an "open text," where new combinations and meanings emerge from the reader's improvisational recontextualizing. Like many works of Language poetry—perhaps most chiefly those by Hejinian, Collom's dear friend and frequent collaborator—such poems make apprehensible the navigational patterns of the reader orienting herself within complex linguistic flows. For Collom, these investigations into the syntax of perception (and vice versa) are less oriented by the engagements with literary theory and Marxist politics that characterize Language poetry's political poetics, however. Instead, they examine the complex semiotics of language in and as ecology. In this way, Collom draws Language poetry's strategies out into the field.

Collom's field-poetics, in turn, gather insight and strategy from Black Mountain poetries, with their attention to the unit of the breath and the spatial dimensions of the page. The influence of these techniques can be felt in poems like "4/22/16/Earth Day" from this volume, which scatter phrases across the page to the tempo of an observation as it develops:

House finch song dances
      Across the back alley
                              into the
            blue-white sky   also
                              white blossoms
      blow in from the left
                                    house sparrows
                  *chirp

Tracking the phenomenological qualities of a moment as it unfolds, Collom's poem charts layers of perception, alert to simultaneities, durations, unexpected turns. Here, the asterisk marks one such turn, the sparrows' sharp tone punctuating the softer song and motion of the scene. Many of Collom's pieces can be understood as field-compositions in this sense, word-graphs of the ever-changing interplay of active mind and surround. A devoted birdwatcher for most of his life, Collom imbues his poems with keen awareness of the rhythms, songs, and habitat of bird life, as the poem above beautifully conveys.

Collom's writing life bears a longstanding connection to Naropa University, where he taught for over thirty years. Naropa's dual legacies of Buddhism and Beat poetics, particularly its principles of care for the earth and attentiveness to everyday rituals of presence, inflect Collom's work in various ways. At the same time, Naropa's poetics curriculum has been indelibly shaped by Collom's creative pedagogy. Through his pioneering course on Eco-Lit, which he taught for twenty years at Naropa, Collom elaborated a unique approach to eco-poetry, drawing together environmental literature, fieldwork, and innovative poetic practices. The first such course of its kind, this class forged a new path for a generation of poetic practitioners and has been often imitated by other teachers of ecopoetics. This course, which draws students into dialogue with various ecological and experimental modes of composition while also bringing them out to Boulder's foothills and hiking trails, might be understood as a collective enactment of Collom's own eclectic, engaged practice of ecopoetics.

It is Collom's formative work in eco-poetry for which he is most widely known, and where his most expansive poetic influence might be felt. His ecological vision can be said to unite these various threads of his poetic practice. Offering a expansive and intricate vision of ecological relationality, Collom's eco-poetry is at once attentive to the local and to wider dimensions of natural relations—planetary, evolutionary, geological. Collom infuses his poems with observations of the Colorado landscape, from the local cultural fixtures of Boulder (Dot's Diner, the Boulderado) to the dirt roads, granite and sandstone rocks, steep canyons, and the complex bird, animal and plant life of the area. These poems also scale out to vaster biospheric processes, back to the long history of earthly life, and inward to the smallest units of matter. They reflect on the intensifying conditions of biospheric crisis, from climate change to habitat loss, urbanization to fracking, while also insisting on nature's capacity for regeneration amidst these ongoing transformations. Above all, Collom draws forth, again and again in his poetry, the fundamental symmetries between natural and linguistic complexity. In their participatory openness to their surroundings, Collom's poems do not merely describe ecological systems but *embody* their entangled, ongoing interconnections. In so doing, they model a form of extended awareness of ecological being and a devotion to the natural world in its manifold presences.

Collom's eco-poetry has had enormous influence on subsequent generations of ecologically-minded poets. From his voluminous creative work to his manifestos to his pedagogical practices, Collom's example is a guiding inspiration for the burgeoning turn to ecopoetics in contemporary poetry today. The publication of this new volume alongside the wonderfully capacious *Red Car Goes By: Selected Poems, 1955-2000* (Tuumba Press, 2001) and *Second Nature* (Instance Press, 2012), which won the 2013 Colorado Book Award, will further solidify Collom's position as an essential figure of experimental ecopoetics.

Yet it is perhaps Collom's extensive collaborative projects that best reflect the fundamental principles motivating his life's work (and life's play) in poetry. He has written poems and books with writers such as Lyn Hejinian, Elizabeth Robinson, Elizabeth Willis, Reed Bye, and Larry Fagin, among others. This volume contains several such collaborations, along with a series of pieces written with his daughter, Sierra. Collom also engaged in sustained collaborative work through his extensive teaching in the public schools in Colorado, New York, Idaho, and other states. (I was fortunate enough to have been a student of Collom's as a third-grader at Martin Park Elementary School in Boulder in the late 1980s. We wrote a poem about birds and a collaborative piece on poetry as a class. I remember it as my first real encounter with poetry; it was utterly enthralling!) The fruit of such endeavors can be discovered not only in the volumes Collom wrote on teaching poetry to children, his anthologies of children's poetry, and the collaborative poems gathered here and in other books, but in the awakening to poetry that he fostered in students over several decades. This legacy of collaborative service also continues in the Project Outreach program he helped establish at Naropa, which brings Naropa students into schools, homeless shelters, prisons, and other locations to teach.

What all these practices have in common is a devotion to poetry as an active encounter with another, a way of being, thinking, and making together in language. Poetry is always a form of social communication in Collom's work, one that emerges from intimate, inductive engagement with others (human and nonhuman). Poetry is a gift, a gesture, a form of dialogue extended over time and space. It is a means of staying alert to the ceaseless diversity of living, in each moment, in a dynamic and responsive environment.

Across his varied body of work, Collom practices an aesthetics of generosity and receptiveness to the creative energies of earthly life. Discovering poetry in all manner and matter of existence, Collom spurs his readers to "keep looking."

Margaret Ronda is an associate professor in the Department of English at the University of California-Davis, where she teaches American poetry and environmental theory and literature. She is the author of Remainders: American Poetry at Nature's End, *as well as two books of poems,* Personification *and* For Hunger.

SELF-PORTRAIT

PREFACE
Jack Collom

Quick history (of me—excuse: the writings are what they are partly for personal reasons).

Born Chicago, 1931. Raised in small town nearby, & the forest preserves. Walks and books, and language humors. A couple of friends.

Poetry as given in middle school: "point out the metaphor."

Wrote my only childhood poem at age 11; crude burlesque of Poe's "Raven." Inspired by the spooky lingo (rather than the bird).

Though I was and am an impassioned birdwatcher.

Moved to Colorado (with family) at 15. High school grad class of 4 kids, high mountain town of Fraser.

Shy, bright (offbeat), woodsy.

Wildlife Management major. Colorado A&M.

1954 Korean War, joined USAF to beat the draft.

Made friends with artloving bunch of airmen.

Started writing. First poems (age 23) Tripoli, Libya, 11 in one day (mediocre, self-absorbed, good rhythm). Noticed I was discovering (not simply recording) what I knew. Kept on.

Post-USAF, NYC, Lower East Side, ('56), lived with painter friend and his wife. They said I should be a poet. Began 20 years of factory work / poetry. Eventually, aided by 2 GI-bill English degrees, I began teaching (freelance, all ages), have done so 40+ years.

Home's mostly been Boulder, CO. A little NYC & Munich, Germany. 3 marriages (the present one with Jennifer Heath for 32 years now). 4 kids.

Early-soaked-up Gerard Manley Hopkins is my favorite poet. Others: Shakespeare, G. Stein, Charles Olson & the "New American Poets," WCW, experimenters, many others.

Variety's the basic fact.

Poetry's a natural. Contra-diction.

It's the music (but never stop there).

February 2017

PART I

OUT

(These lines were written *pre-poetry* in 1954, Greenville, South Carolina. Just exploring)

Rippling stanchions to the contrary, Elbert Hubbard strikes
whomsoever castles his rook, inters his living raven, or dies agog.
Fifteen men on a dead man's chest; yo, ho, ho, and a jereboam
of arak—think! Mates! On the futility of topaz eyelets.
Notice the constant demands made of any ulterior hummingbird.
And then ask me wherefore thousands of unemployed auklets seek
to discover who runs the southern rivers.
But should we find, amidst our wanderings, that all is not
sane … what then?
And if you are not such a prepossessing rum-brewer as Captain
Marks, I deem it a sorry extension of philistinic node
that you continue in your adopted vein.
But, it has been said, he who draws fire into his nostrils
shall become as the minor gods in all ways but one.
As a ten o'clock scholar, he withered serenely all the month
long—waiting for who knows what change of inner liquid.
Half of the knaves in Lichtenstein are those citizens who
delve unconcernedly into the pots boiled up by their left-
hand neighbors, and half are not.
A dancing Weltzchmerz runs silently but hackles frequent
abortive eruptions from lo! below the surging deeps, eh?
Filaments of iceberged fury charging relentlessly into the
Cave of the Winds would be a sorry prospect indeed, consi-
dering the thousands upon thousands of hoary bats depen-
dent on federal handouts for education and highway cons-
truction.
And furthermore, though many a tangle-haired sailor has braved
the pullulating quintessence of the succession of faunal
broths indigenous to the southern tip of the Malayan Penin-
sula, no thinking wombat could conceivably shine at quoits.

EQUALS

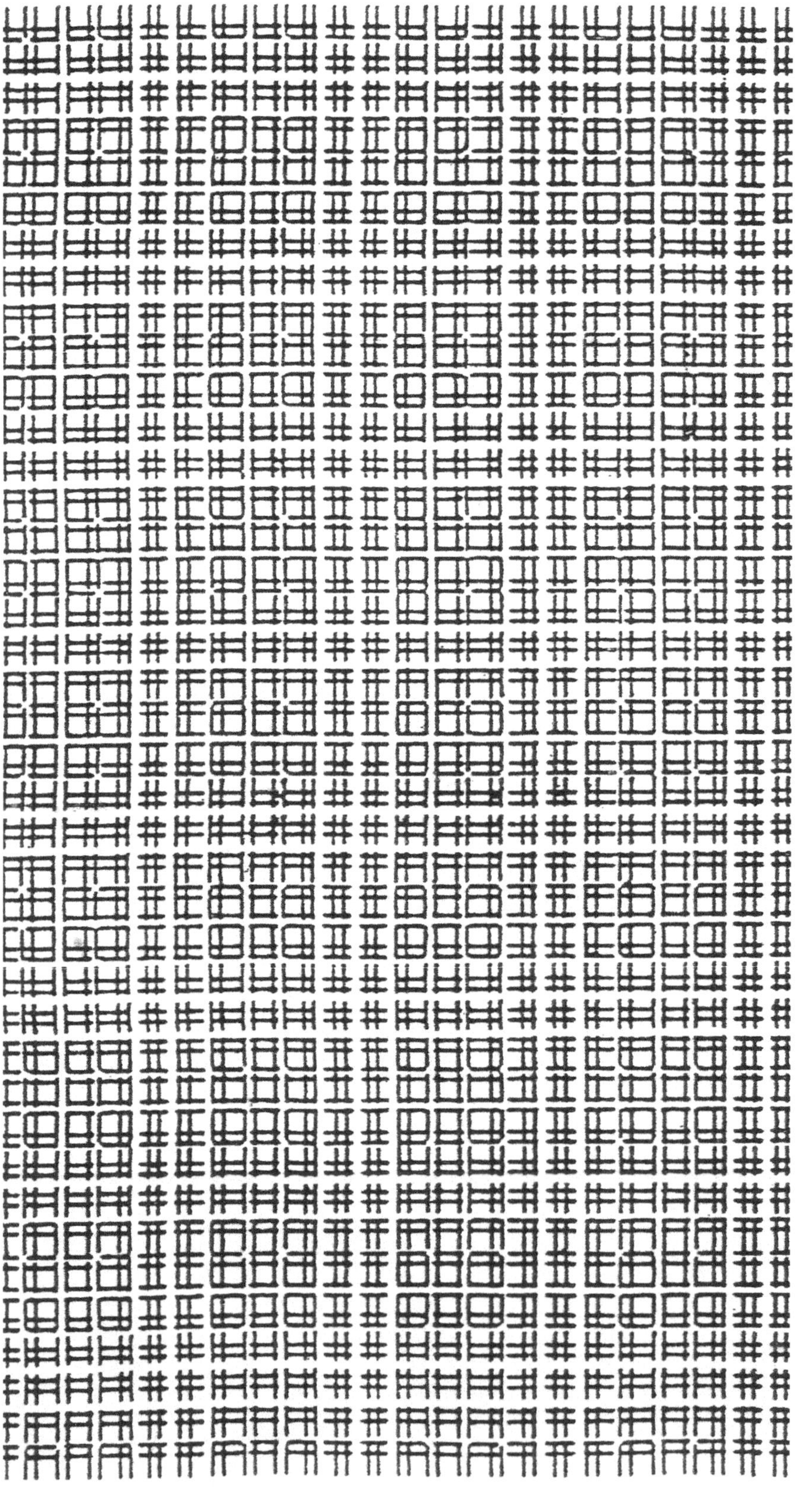

IN OUR FAMILY

in our family
like striking matches for the Indians to wear
we say many things
like a compliment that comes almost to everybody
& the air is full of their remains
like blowing the air out of it
would precipitate a floor of kindness
with a fort full of sugar crust
this is always the empty room
like tempenning a queer marketain
so vivid is the presence of the small people
printing the portrait I found
in the bed all over the walls
no tempenning person has heard of
because he cannot but see through them
like suggesting your time
can't be broken since it's all a point
of tastering a frog
until the green blows up
tiny sparkles of god
penetrating the near earth
as can't surviving the same word I said
clear below to hold everything up
as ending the story I told you
a flat beginning
twenty-one endings of a story
is only a start because the space
becomes on your lives
a complete dizziness
as scampering all ends of a story
into a box will only lead to death

Jack Collom with son Chris Collom (age 7)

RIVERTREE 12 1965

bedd wrough

bread wreath

breath

crax breathe breed thee

break breeth

wrea brak blead deathe

rak

sough sourh

stough gloe

slough shan

PHRASE RIVERTREE, LOVE 11-27-67

before I can to establish a tough

keeping it dry as it happens

the murder of blue a heaviness noted

as the silence would be her regular

continuing the plan the turning silver of a face

and if it doesn't seem I quickly eat

while water somewhere resembling a machine

mere size in the hands accomplish their

scream an outline of the basic field

and before I can

Josh Lerman, grandson, age 6

1961

saprophyte Willy?
why don't we turk rapid filet
downstream? hack,
Baden-Baden really snaps art meal flap
after four but which
actual to snip apt marvel big scot
let's try it warmly fly loose
butter lucid purple spill donations
sorry we peal mentira
wallaby flee or april-play-badly

duck splint

carnival

retract

lard

Papa macht ca-ca
Natty watches Papa as
plays smashface me identifies
Nat sociable runs red cross car on radiator
wipe ass
its parts plus coffee, ashtray
closes door a measure against stink
living-room ah Christopher
as Kilidoodle gets pen I
Toddl-u has taught him
safe, Nat 2 guns stretched my
provide paper but you must bring
Papa macht Koppl (burp)
lap urgency up:
chair back to table eventually OK
minor glory of the German tongue
Nurry! at door, well
Nat with raisins I again coffee
flips ash in catbox Natty righteously
get down so I can get up and
hmm Christopher
No! Nurry! and a long explanation
let her in, Ach so/Nat
alone on the couch dissatisfied
understandable Nurry aagghh:
tries to shoot Papa poetry
Papa fetches puts on leg now
That is where Nurry
point-blank
quiet leaning over my
does distastefulness
points barrel protests that I fill every
little spiral notebook amazing
perform
space here/do I not?/Natty
wiggles leaving fast blue doodle
Orangehead
in lines light mewls astonsihed contentment
anthropomorphi-
cize/automatic drool when tipped a
principle of biophysics
demand pen of Natty when not
at table Nat deny puts it back
obeying yet saving face
Toddle-u awake I start
himself for her Nat
goes back to wrestle and ha ha
thus
a new era begins

quietly tears me down at this time
(ah slug of hot coffee) I
(the animals House of the Rising Sun)
but quietly leave quietly drive
(odd people around me)

delicious cups of coffee.
fan noticeable now.
odd people settling.
bright machines, fan, telephone, ringing,
false brick, in the basement
PALE ORANGE
on a pipe
the Miller High Life ad
as I drove
in dark I desired to return to

desired to return to

desired to return to
make peace with, love Natty put him to
bed be friends

scanty real color this evening

unsatisfying sound
time for luminous twilight
which slipped by all too soon

I was born to drink coffee in U.S. cafes.
I am six foot three

gravitate sidewalkwise
seat Revelation—yes Bright
light to write
by buzz Danger live wire neon
Orange Glow Laborious Spaghetti
bzzz trash behind dangling with guts phone book soft from stiff back
hot cup Real brick hemmed in formica
comes to an end I
will always sit here,
when I come get out now coffee lousy too fast cools
quick before cool crumble ugh, ah,
fresh black air
unwittingly lit up
marquee changing "Chi a!"
ass full of gas
THE END IS NEAR back home

aside from that it snowed a little last night

out of ascendancy

Tom's taste

all this maniac perception

hang on to
outmoded figure I do differ
in some burden of human

colors and humors
unclinical if you please

robin unaware chirping dadgum human
in the snow

some tatted thing under a white thing that holds
we move soon in-
to my watercolors here

drive to work sometimes through
dangerous sunlight the immediate hills
covered with frost only the great slabs of rock
not, positively
brown light-embedded in that
elegance

There. Two hours of assembly and
87 pyrex leak stems
in the furnace purge time by
while I peed now up with the voltage
to 950°C pretty hot where
they'll flow naturally the H_2
I sit
like some gruff captain with his wheels

goddamn smooth and light around
me all repugnantly:
pulling their puds getting through the day
sweat
rubbing oxidation off
smoked oysters for lunch to alienate
how alien Monday I am
aware/the leak stems seem to
be mostly leakers, delicate propositions
trying running up again the
little pieces of gunmetal gray tube glued together with real gold
and the gold seemed
it is patchy leave holes

6 a huge yellow blast through the
kitchen window that's the sun
shooting on a level with me now

knocking me back against the icebox just enough
filling the house coffee left 3-pound can of Max-

bup
diba
time to move bubadabl bop
uba babbl dip dubble bup

Orangehead licking herself on the big green papa chair

Ha, some day old rye bread
20¢
we are nearing
the solution of the problem of the leak stems
theories abound/perhaps
the wrong monel one that
can only be brazed in a dry hydrogen
atmosphere, and of course the
glassing kovar needs a wet, perhaps
something we may call dirt was left
on the belled part
by the pickle or the temperature was wrong
too low it didn't flow too high it drained out
here comes that damn music again
discovered another bad
mistake of mine too many lately
feel low, and scared,
at coffee, think seriously of cutting off
a finger to go with my tattoo etc
look down my left hand it seems
so strong and able there ending my arm
my spirit/
eight-inch bland butterscotch
dark and light/glowing lemon-yellow
diaper pot white-topped like a frosty
towels colors of:
fake green tile shielding the tub
obnoxious little; rubber, anin
a vision -! The toilet won't flush (fact)
lifted the cake off and mindless
crowded blue leap to 9 pm. reached in that maze of mechanery pulled
Traudl movie something up not knowing/it was correct
put Nat to bed he'd fallen asleep ont worked, fixed through blindness

the couch   of the mind's eye pork
while I was taping crowded blue oldsteak ice (potatoes) salad and beets
and he   instant coffee
was wild almost epileptic I was afraid wet chocolate dust
coughed up brown stuff from excess
screams   feel all thumbs
poor bruised boy never did wake up   of mind and soul
the whole change   with that blue-brown bone-crunching/
/
/no just a dark
/cloud of elbows
of the blues people and the old jazz
flailing the decade
out of any place
my
abstract
glass-
blowing/shining by ribbon under the light
abstract water-colors taped on the door
pencil drawings   photos saved I made   scrap metal coll???
tion curtains open
black air out there

beautiful windows of the neighbors

gold tapestries pale blue rectangles

words
words
words
words
words
words
words
words
words
words
words
words
words
words
words
words
words
words
words
words
words
words
words
words
words
words
words
words
words
words
words
words
words
words
words
words
words
words
words

Nathaniel Collom, age 7

time is an enemy
thick air
a pigeon writes
c
& out
Frost
Dog bones
chris shows me a note nat wrote
"jack is a fucker love nat"
mindlove morning
love—get rid of it
saying: it's done
the dog chews bones
love
leaps in instantly
wave or particle
light fucks frost
smoke
each thing, a thing
how about the light
invisible but works?
dawn
is almost gone
the slant
bong a peak
bear peak there
all day long
lucky
frostlight lucky mindlove
got kaka in your pants, 'quoya?
Uh-unh
8:25 squint against the sun
looking at the slight
wave of the southeast horizon
hiding Denver blue on blue
a little sparkle left
in the yard

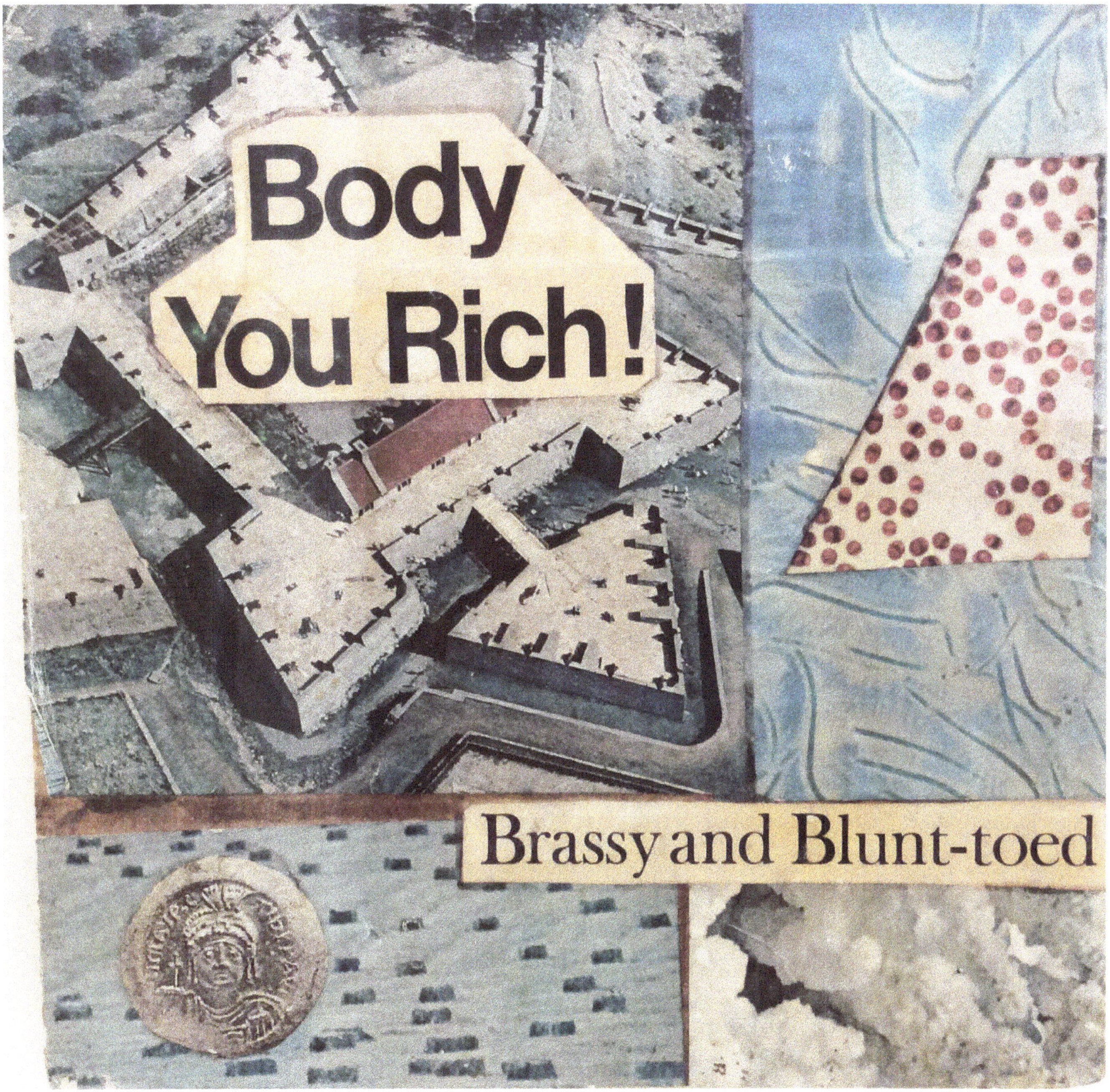
Body
You Rich!
Brassy and Blunt-toed

LE BAR 12-27-79

why would a man named john with an eternal sailor cap, a ramshackle
bohemian with Russian eyes and lavender latinate talk, leave a
little chunk of hamburger and some chips while he draws left-
handed mystical and exotic pictures, leave them in a red-white
checkered cardboard box, sauce, too, why leave them, here, in
the Boulderado hotel as I sit sipping my club soda with lime
15 minutes off work, IBM second shift, hot rolls, and
drove through a big soft blizzard—why leave them, after his
adventures in cutting the bread, in dark places, while I look
upon it as if it were a sable antelope viewed through the wrong
end of a telescope while the wind blows up from the waterhole?
oh, he didn't, he ate them and is mumbling
let us go off into, yes, yellow
ness, of the shape, no, after blue
wandering-through stick-men something their cereal, on horses which
are 3-dimensional and kind
light sags into the lower part of the scene
a sash passes up and down
they turn white in a soft-shine forward-and-back dance
where do we go? Off to the right there is a city
when we arrive we are taken for crooked kings
we get down in the street and fry some eggs—"see how you are?"

It might be that we are all tattooed savages since Sophocles.
.A world not conceived by an absolute-- shattered: on a book.%
(Sometimes Foucault globally rejects the language of reason.)
The analyst must utilize the same language as the patient.
(We would have to choose, then, between writing and dance.)
*Better still when letters are no longer figures of fire.!
(Structure is perceived through the incidence of menace.)
(Crises of reason in complicity with crises of madness.*
*I have tried to-attempt-to-say-the-demonic-hyperbole.!
?Have we fully understood the sign itself, in itself??
@Each noema supposes possibility of noema generally.@
(There is no insurance against the risk of writing.)
(Meaning becomes meaning by differing from itself.*
&There is a transcendental & preethical violence.&
!Of madness itself. Itself. Of madness itself.#
-I assume that the greek logos had no contrary.-
(Of general censorship of the text in general!)
1First of all, is there a history of silence?0
2Along the lines of the Hegelian Entzweiung.1
.The enigma of presence "pure and simple":.-
0"A universe to be added to the universe."0
-Grace can only be that which is missing.-
(The essential shadow of the undeclared.)
½Between the explicit and the implicit.½
!Parched woman drinking the inky dust.!
.Unified foundations of dissociation.0
#Syntax, or, if you will, its labor.@
-Freud set them off against poetry.-
-Beauty, which is value and force.-
-A certain sin of explicationism.%
-But metaphor is never innocent.-
."Behold, here is a new table."-
-Space of the stage of dreams.-
(Servile matter or excrement.#
Husserl has been sensitive.
.Be an object (Gegenstand)..
-If it recedes one day....-
(Books live on aloneness.)
&Invoking an energetics.*
½In praise of Dionysus?!
-Writing is inaugural.-
(Space of repression.)
-La parole soufflée.-
$Fill his entrails.$
1Noncontradiction.1
#Enigma of flesh.#
-If we consider.-
Lapsus calami.
:Act of force.!
*For example.:
"The Savage."
Bricolage.
(Formless.)
-Overlap.)
.Infant.+
/Signs!/
%Play.%
(Etc.)
(Ad.)
(8.)
(.)
()

JACQUES DERRIDA

WRITING AND DIFFERENCE

Memory

(for Mark Twain)

Friend of mind plays "Red-headed Stranger" all the time,
Admires the all-purpose outlaw voices.
Featured on that album is a version of
"Remember Me," which song I first heard in 1948
from the recorded lips of T. Texas Tyler.
And, back then, when the Fraser, Colorado, high school basketball team
had played Central City
& we were driving back to Fraser over Berthoud Pass, the
whole team crammed into the '39 LaSalle of Lambert Howell,
who ran the sawmill off into the woods from Hideaway, in which I
incidentally tailed the planer the following summer,
working with an old boy with about three teeth in his head
named Frank Lafarlatte, who was illiterate, & whose wife
had recently made her living hanging by her teeth
from a trapeze bar in the circus—I remember

riding into Denver with them one time,
stopping in Idaho Springs for some coffee, & Frank
surprising me by visually picking out about 1 mph
"Pee-Wee-Hunt" on the jukebox—there was also an
Old pearshaped guy named Honeycutt there,
which I thought for months was his nickname due to the
chewing tobacco he always let dribble down his white stubble
so he had two ovals of amber on his chin
— he had *no* teeth—but it was his *name—and* in which
a young feller named Marvin Quick had the crackerjack job,
sawyer—Marvin had just married Betty Rae Radebaugh,
who'd been a sophomore in high school that year & who
flirtatiously waited tables in Clayton's Café.
anyway, when Lambert Senior
was driving us all back from Central City to Fraser—
& by the way Lambert was one of the most amazing drivers
I ever saw: he'd logged over a million miles driving
trucks all around the Rockies—he could take the canyon
between Kremmling and Hot Sulphur Springs at 100 miles per
in that old LaSalle & make it feel like laying on a featherbed—
anyway, having heard T. Texas Tyler sing, "Remember Me,"
with that special growl on the title words, I was singing,

"Remember me, when the candlelight is gleaming,"
with a huge growl, over & over, probably jammed between
Lambert Junior & Jack Leonard (our star) or (gulp)
Marilyn Tucker in the back seat, I forget who won the game,
& Lambert Senior said, "Waaal now, how could I forget you?"
snow piled on the sides of the passing road.
                                                            The very next year,
student at State A & M, I *saw* T. Texas Tyler, with his colored
shirt & devilish thin lips, sing "Remember Me,"
smirking & looking off-beat, & also recite
his famous deck-of-cards thing, where the deck in his
shirt pocket stops a bullet & gets translated into
biblical allegory, layer by layer.

MIX-DISPENSE 4-5-79

running rust-colored rubber
onto metal paint-sprayed ethereal pink
and pressing it up through silver molds
dark-yellow-plastic-capped

frosty-looking bushes star the
costly landscape between the brown wings
of IBM boulder—second shift sunset
begins to light up a few evergreens

gravel lines the pale sidewalk to the
great parking lot—a supervisor named Schmidt
walks it: long sideburns, martini face &
springy progress like an aging carousel.

SNOWBALL 11-27-75

awoke at six feeling blue
up & dressed & out for a walk, almost dark
coffee & breakfast, returned;
presents for 2-year-old sierra: a snowball in her warm tub
& honey locust pod
for mara: intricate weed & 1961-62
texas almanac

now drinking tecate listening to locatelli
l'arte del violin reading excellent texas geography,
mara dresses sierra
in green & orange

sunny, clear sky

tv cartoon stills of righthanded Leonardo
with rhetorical narration
play hank williams "rosewood casket"
thanksgiving
morning—oatmeal sierra

I took s. for two walks
got some good beer from all over the world
& catfood & shermans at the cornucopia
on our way
back

walking in the alley we
spied a small bird just in line
with the light gray crescent moon
finch "dipped in strawberry
waters"
blood on the moon
when he turned

& we walked on over
the tormented snow & dirt of the alley
home

the snowball in warm tub went
with a kind of lickety-split quietude
to ice & out
& clear out

3-9-79

changing chains on reduction 64
that won't get finished cuz the kid
fucked up the masterlink setting,
about to leave it in R-1, slop Gojo
on my black hands & go punch out …
the kid pontificating, small in his blond
halo & Transylvanian fangs, malaise cuz
confronted by lack of an external referee,
& by gum his love thing don't work out …
D.J. turns to me & says, "shit,
man, I ain't never seen such
cognitive dissonance in my motherfucking life."

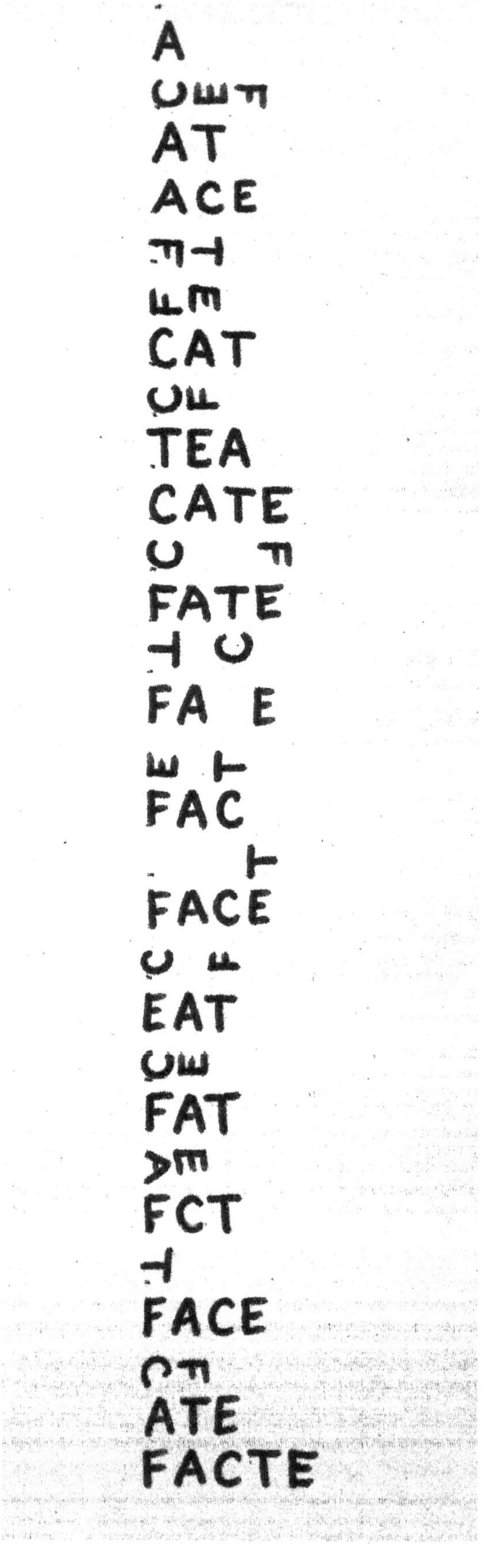
A
AT
ACE
CAT
TEA
CATE
FATE
FA E
FAC
FACE
EAT
FAT
FCT
FACE
ATE
FACTE

moose cash register

sonic happy eating

embudito

sizzler

midas

mountain view meat market

faith growth

foot specialist

mountain view meat market

foot specialist

moon mart

moon mart

cloth world

midas

sizzler

embudito

moose cash register

sonic happy eating

abc chinese

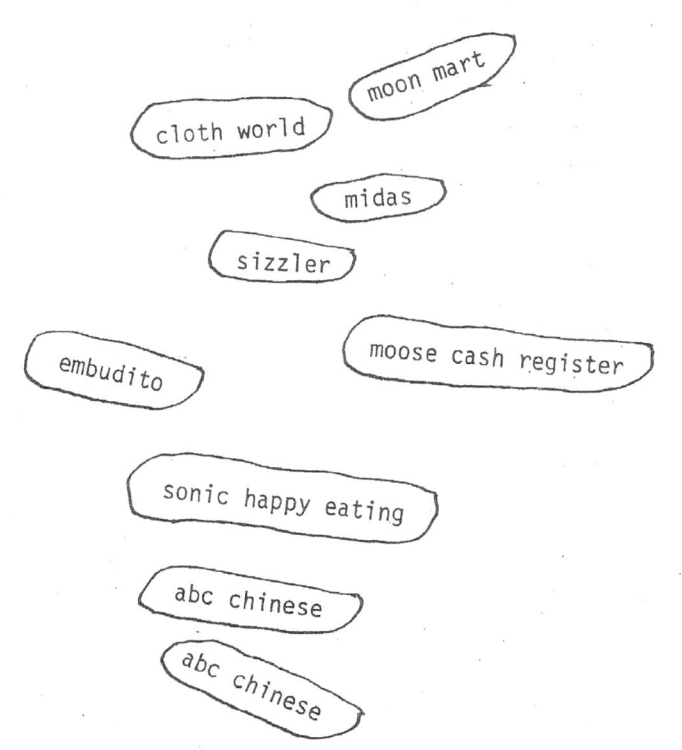

abc chinese

financing provided by

another byte

wild bird center ♈

cash pawn

financing provided by

sale pending

dr. jack zipper

lieber's luggage

enlightenment center

shocks · struts

one executive center

sundance

vet-co

cimarron square

pump 'n save

baby furniture ♈

king

soccer locker ♈

diehard service

sale pending ♈

HOT WINGS

POEM

Slant Opposites

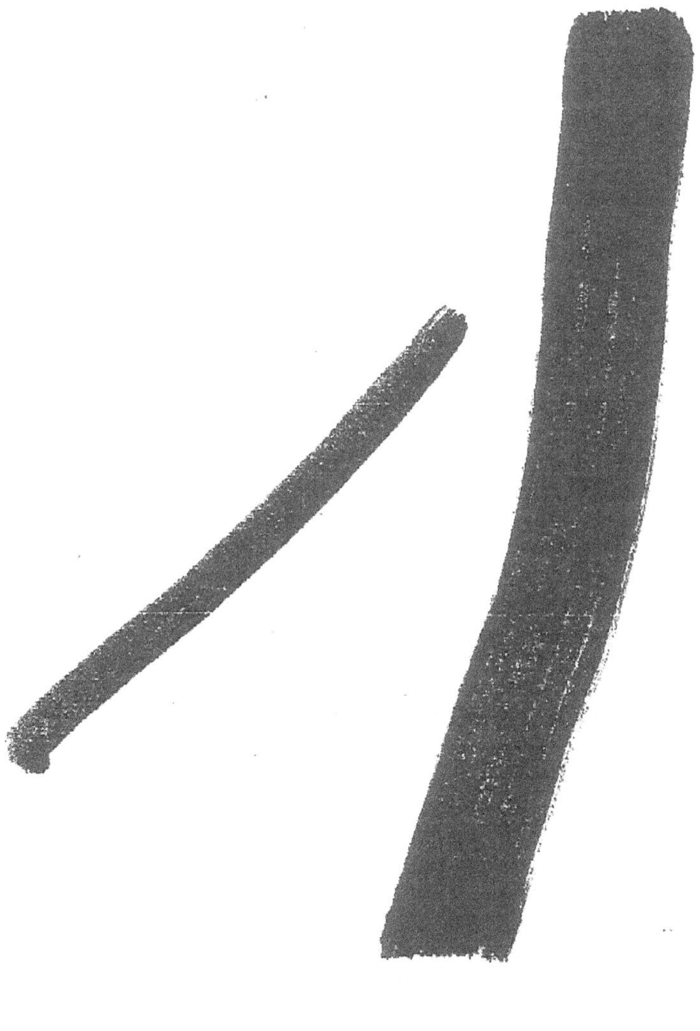

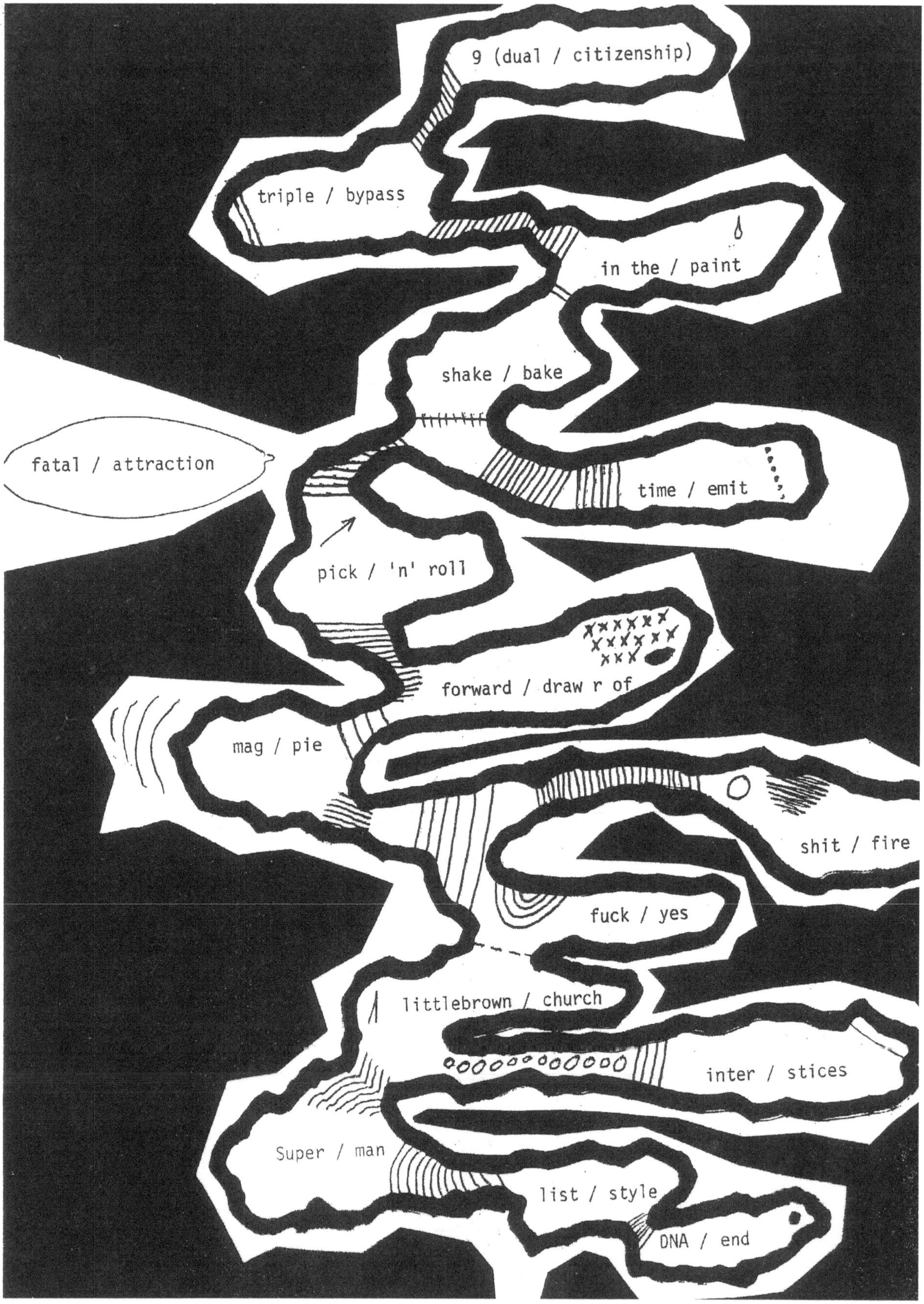
9 (dual / citizenship)
triple / bypass
in the / paint
shake / bake
fatal / attraction
time / emit
pick / 'n' roll
forward / draw r of
mag / pie
shit / fire
fuck / yes
littlebrown / church
inter / stices
Super / man
list / style
DNA / end

POSTKATHMANDU 6-30-06

Wilderness Information Next Door
more books, oh boy
Speed Limit 35 what
is that you're eating?
whereas *your* eating is
impeccable as a sandpiper
the clouds are drifting
eastward into our lines
two curves heading away
into you, my deer
the dirt road blues
under blue eyeshadow sky
you've got icewater in your
truck, I hope
look—a white car
with washboard meadow music
thirty mailboxes for forty
happy cowboys living high
Magnolia Road's upper melody
lower limit jackalope note
ponderosa pay-as-we-go yes? no
blow me down easy
passing Merrill's loggerhead shrike
wired half-song fell down
aspen too complicated to
draw, too easy to
crow about—opening up
into scrub, red truck
goes by as if
it had anywhere to
be a part of
of trucks, I say
little but I sing
as loudly as possible
over the hump and
guardrails feverfews, valley paintbrush
yellow lines of talk
open space for sale
sand and exploding greenery
skillful braking by pilot

harmony with popping eats
going down faster closer
lovely distances, details too
bent arrow heading east
past pinecone club gatherings
red jawlike rock veins
song of first gear
set against condo rising
and water treatment plant
slow side road traffic
Silver Spruce, keep out
netting rocks for you
grooved centerline next 4
stream crossed wooden bridge
down in the canyon
sand in your shoes
and in your shoes
here we are again
almost The Red Lion
tired hiker, sweaty beard
purple thistle swimming hole
what happened to the
as a prefix or
a housing project that
became almost completely specific
against a geologic mind
look at that jumble
on the jumble sigh
we break into prairie
and into city maintenance
which will endure for
as long as we don't come to a
catastrophic failure to stop
or an ordinary stop sign

by Elizabeth Willis and Jack Collom

BREAK 8-21-90

I'm sitting at one of those old purple-brown picnic tables.
The air's dotted with west-flowing "cotton."
I face a grassy field half-melted by morning light
Occasional cars buzz & flash, half-hidden, by, up Sunshine Canyon.
Behind the road's a ponderosa hill leading to Little Red Rocks.
However, Little Red Rocks can't be seen, just the blue and white sky.
A willow, to my right, arches branches across that sky, & across the phone
    wires that horizontally divide it.
Two pieces of "cotton" blow dumbly about the newspaper on which I've placed
    my writing paper.
Behind me's the white noise of an 18-inch-wide brook falling over a thick log.
A path edges around my back & heads upstream, through creekbottom woods.
A few yards left of me stands a brick shelterhouse.
Above it, a fox squirrel travels branches toward me, veers away north.
A lady in very light blue, with sunglasses, retrieves her bicycle & departs.
A peach pit lies in the path.
Birdshit and a couple yellow willow leaves adorn the table.
Two red ants explore the tabletop, through areas of yellow dirt & carved
    names, such as "Noah."
A discarded or lost bandaid lies in the shadow of the table.
Hikers emerge, talking, down from Mt. Sanitas Trail.
Two park rangers come nosing by.
The hum of a nearby generator becomes apparent.

PART II

Bunches

several
groups
of
poems

MID-1960S

Twilight paper

W O
R M

XMAS WEEK AT THE BRASS MILL 1961

Once again
I work with low lead, zinc, nickel hooks,
weld rod, makeup engraver's
copper, barrel bronze, antimony, 4-K fortifier,
compound no. 4,
cartridge brass, red and yellow pickles, roll
depolarized nickel anodes, keystock,
resistant
wire, tough pitch, rich
low brass, Fourdrinier,
special white, gliding and
grain silver

—

RIVERTREE 18

boustrophedon red-hot

phaleron egg

telephones

avalanche ice marlborough marrowbone

catechism totempole

bugs bel canto amber erector set

anteater

rosebud steak

australia sea horse

centuries finger

TAKEN BREATH

well here
we are back in
the old thing
variety
sun & shadow
etc. all those
interacting pairs—the days
in sum
baroque

can't stop
remembering
love
the unbearable classic
carried fire
fact

nor meaning
as that can be
to keep it in
& more possible
renew it as
ground of function
hard replacement
gets on too fast

the worm in mud
that gets hard too
 & breaks
a wing lies out of

nor getting ground
to keep kindling it in—what
coldness
simple passing is
accumulates
something pulled?
builds
a "wall" without

real question
to

but mind
called split off
does reconnoiter for the anchor
half before & after this
holds
what
this depends on
is rubbed out by

body too

cause

SONG

my finger
made of light
(this must surprise me too
or be no singing)
dipped in person
bleeds
I lick it up
spectrum
moves in cells
absence
more generally
what
does that mean love

yeah

—

danger

the moon
is
cold and remote as me

earth's brown
seems set
below

the grass
is bright green
no one in sight

PARADOX
paradox
PARADOX
PARADOX
PARADOX
PARADOX

TWO WEEKS in PARADOX

Jan. 2001

seems to be
imposi-
ble
but is play

UP AT 5, down at 5:15
in the City of Boulder
pack up, out kiss good-bye

WHAT IS TROOTH?
IT IS NOTHING
BUT THE TROOTHE.

predawn/ internal/ combustion
out, along prairie-hills
in the dark to Golden

PARADOX.

I-70 X
screeches durch (thru) the Rockies
Idaho Springs

UP, UP &

winter strikes
fire at Ike Tunnel
through, no light

Q: Why is the sky blue?
A: Dust.
Q: Dust?
A: That...
Q: That?
A: That & light.
Q: Just light?
A: Unjust.
Q: Unjust like waves?
A: Partly.

down the mountain
stop and piss
yellow into white equals black

over the pass to Vail
snow, off the interstate to pee otra vez
touch brake
00000!

spin
around parked bus, slam
into snow pile
-- @@@@ --
wham.
quiescent phalanx of ski-bums
(O Knights of the Long Board)
waiting for me

dig me out, pull me
out, labor, refuse money
wave, and fingerwag: "slow"

SCIENTISTS CLAIM
HUMAN SPEECH IS
LIKE FLURRIES OF SNOW.

down to Eagle (open), then
down Glenwood /---/ to Glenwood O
sticky whiteness slide

slick town -- no stop here
but gas up, soon (I think
as I peer back through blackness of tomorrow)

constant music
on (off?) tape, jolly
Depression tunes of pain & sorrow

hard & soft Good
(bread, peanutbutter,
carrots, hot sauce) en passant

MY GOODNESS --
YELLOW LIGHT SAGS
BELOW SKIRT! somewhere

diet Coke
(time stuck together
with fact, like spirit rr. track)

SILT, RIFLE

finally: Grand Junction arrives
Atlas speaks /// still
120 miles to go

south into wild canyons
open roads & icy spots
skirting the Uncompahgre Plateau

clusters of crows
around crunched animals
scatter as I come

stop, in Gateway
tiptoe through the ice
for muffin & coffee

ANYBODY COULD WRITE
THIS. BUT
NOBODY ELSE DID!

served by dark children
the-
re *in the store*

roll on roll on
(roll on)
"Paradox Right"

straight line

just before Paradox
stop -- Bedrock store
gaze at the Red Cliffs north

& consider the Dolores
River that crosses + + +
the valley

MEANWHILE
INTUITION SNAPS
ASH FROM CIGARETTE
AT FIFTY PACES;

(remembering
an hour before
when the highway suddenly

heaved me a thousand feet up
on the rim
<u>sobre</u> Dolores)

INTELLECT
CLOSES THE DOOR
OF THE OUTHOUSE.

through Paradox then
past blood-red church & empty "Paradox"
to Hayes (host) home

tucked in the corner
of Paradox (ically)
oval Valley

juncos flit white
tailstripes into
sage

ALABASTER
FILLS CUP, IS slowly
SMASHED TO SALT.

(sandwich)
phonecalls
supper
talk

rEad paper (Sunday
Daily Camera) plus 2 pages
T. C. Boyle

<u>A Friend</u>
<u>of</u>
<u>the Earth</u>

"LINGUINE"

BARELY EXPRESSES

EVERYTHING I FEEL.

cattle
ready for
the slaughter

... paradox:
puzzle, maze, quandary,
horns of a

dilemma, knot, Irish bull,
asses' bridge, perplexity,
riddle, enigma,

Q: What's a pair o' ducks?
A: Almost everything.

uncertainty, antilogy, in-
congruity, oxymoron,
ambiguity... reversal

BUT I'VE TALKED ABOUT MYSELF
LONG ENOUGH, HOW ARE
YOU??

nonsense,
unthinkability
<u>reductio</u> <u>ad</u> <u>absurdum</u>

up at 5:15
contradictory, self-
contradictory

exercise in bed
stretches in the cold
unintelligible

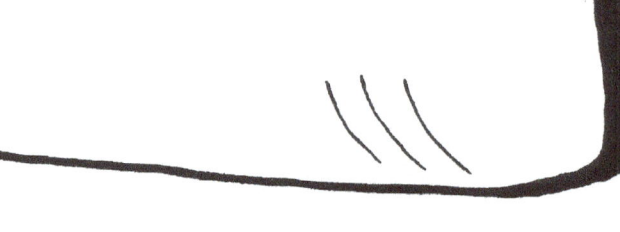

cold instant
coffee (black)
unfathomable

DEEP WITHIN MY HEART
THERE'S A
BABY HEART.

dress up
improbable
write

sandwich breakfast
clean up, out, start car
(lost my scraper) 12 little degrees

drive to school
"THE POET
IS IN" sign colored & hung

VOCABULARY
RUNS AWAY FROM
HOME.

paradox:
from "contrary to
expectation"

<u>para</u>-:
along side of, beyond, aside from,
closely related to, involving
substitution at or characterized by two
opposite positions)(

DON'T FORGET THE DIRT

in the benzene ring
that are
separated by two carbon atoms

faulty
abnormal
subsidiary or accessory
closely resembling

almost,

dokein:
to think, seem
(more at DECENT)

DOGEN?

two opposite positions
in the benzene ring

*a tenet
*contrary to
*received opinion

doggone

heavy cloud cover
silhouette of falcon
on window

AFFECTED FACT
OPTS FOR
FOURTH DIMENSION

"a statement
opposed to common sense
and yet perhaps true"

random swirls
sliced, on
flat brown table

(PARADISE: enclosed park
(("around"
"wall")))

(paralanguage: optional vocal effects ---- TONE OF VOICE
that accompany or modify the phonemes
of an utterance)

150 MILLION YEARS
OF
CANYONLANDS
GEOLOGY

(on the wall)

swing hangs still
sagebrush just sits there
imperturbable mesa shapes

LOCAL
HEADLINE: DISCOVERY DES-
TROYS LIGHT-
NESS.

magpie undulates
across flicker
cry

plastic bag in
wastebasket (that is) painted
battleship gray

ten
of
ten

there's a
subJECtive book
<u>The Hell That Was Paradox</u>

WRIT BY AN OLD COWBOY
WAVING
IN THE DISTANCE.

_/7_ /
O /
( )

Barbara Barnhart arrives
poor dear leader, she's
recovering from Bell's palsy

CHINSTRAP
HUMBOLDT
EMPEROR
LITTLEBLUE

....
Barbara, Renee & I
talk about
school & Paradox

Madame Curie, by the way
found this a hotbed of
radium-soaked petrified wood

in Paris, she & pierre
made initial discoveries
in extracted Paradox "ore"

or:
"WHEN I DIE
I WANNA GO TO
PARADOX."

useta be
packs of gone-wild burros & mules
in the Valley, making a lotta noise at night

Q: Hee?
A: Haw!

the Uranium <u>Boom</u>
brought all kinds of
bizarre oddballs into the area

thus did Moab
never become
a Mormon stronghold

old Charlie Steen
existed in Cisco, scrounged around for poverty years
then struck it rich

lunchtime!

spaghetti
bread cheese cookies chocolate milk (no paradox)

is human nature
contrary to
nature? nature? nature? or

Nucla
Naturita
Uravan

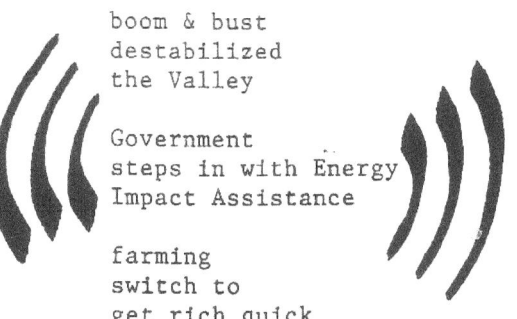

SWINGSET
JUST HANGS THERE. THE CLIFFS
LOOK LIKE FOREVER.

boom & bust
destabilized
the Valley

Government
steps in with Energy
Impact Assistance

farming
switch to
get rich quick

in a sense
tradition is
outlawry

"MY LIFE HAS BEEN A VIOLENT AND BITTER
STRUGGLE AND MY MARRIAGE HAS FALLEN
INTO DECAY. I KNOW THAT FLORENCE IS
LIVING WITH A GAMBLER THAT I HAVE HAD
SEVERAL SCUFFLES WITH OVER THE YEARS.

"ONE IN PARTICULAR WAS IN BUTTE, MONTANA,
WHEN I CAUGHT HIM CHEATING AT CARDS AND
A SHOOTING WAS NARROWLY AVERTED BY THE
INTERVENTION OF THE OTHER PLAYERS."

-- from a conversation with BART YOUNG in 1895

but in a sense, too
modernity brought
fragmented demographics

transients
militant survivalists
trust-fund hippies
no-trust-fund hippies
retirees
fugitives
& nuts like us"

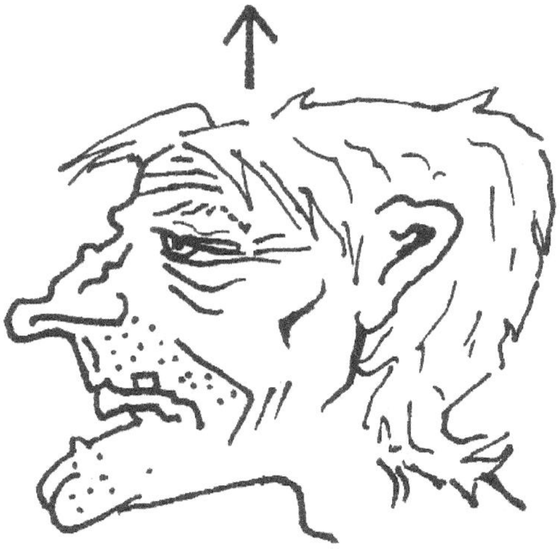

divorces
split the Valley's
length & breadth

mixed bowl
of
loner mentalities

BUREAU OF RECLAMATION
IS DESALINIZING THE
DOLORES RIVER.

Redd Ranches
biggest employer here
sells hybrid bulls

(((((((( ))))))))

((BECAUSE PARADOX IS A
COLLAPSED
SALT DOME))

by pumping salt sludge
three miles straight down
till it tangles with the tectonic plates

/X/X/X/X/

combination of
employment, earthquakes
& broken-window compensation

over west, hole-in-the-rock
settlers
spent a year blasting through

behind Renee's head
hangs reproduction of
Winslow Homer's painting

P EOPLE
O UTSIDE
E YING
T HE
S UPPER.

P aradox
O f
E scalation
T o
S nap, stopped

showing a line of boys
clasping hands, running
across the fields in a mountain valley

zigzag, each one
plunging a bit off balance
"cracking the whip"

their legs forever
framed, forever
scissoring the moment
...

waal, Slim Hecox, now, long ago, at the Cashin Copper
Mine, was bragging on his $3000 -- rash boast --
and someone robbed & decapitated him

CALMLY
STUCK A GUN
THROUGH HIS CABIN WINDOW

At first people couldn't find his head, legend has it, went &
buried him without it, in a short coffin (fit to what they had)
but then they did locate that cabeza somewhere, & dug Slim up

& put the head in the crook of his arm   SINCE IT WOULDN"T FIT
THE REGULAR WAY.

true? nobody knows but it hardly
matters

...

then there was Sew-'Em-Up Mesa, where rustlers would
bring cattle, cut the brand off the living cow,
sew on some new skin & re-brand
after it'd healed up & haired over

...

as far as the school goes,
the regular one was closed down a few years back
lack of students

so the kids had to be driven
all the way to the broken-down broken-up
school over in Naturita

then folks in the West Valley here
paradoxically shed their loner mentalities
got together, started a charter

-- oddly, the childless people
did most of the volunteering
even dumpster-dived for furniture & equipment
pulled things out

***

&
THE
LANDSCAPE
ROLLS
along

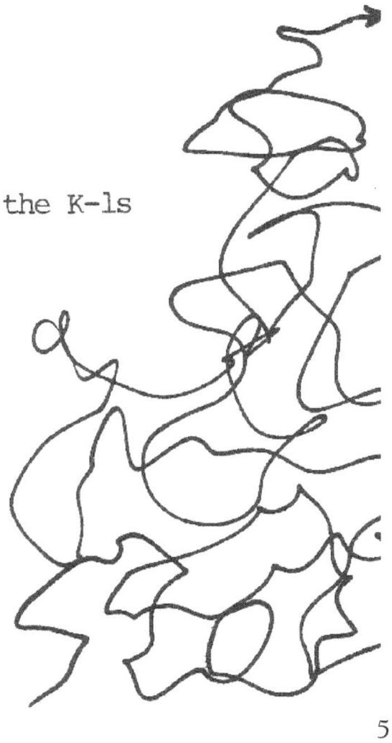

afternoon
3 classes
I-remembers, lunes, Paradox Valley collaboration with the K-1s

teachers meeting, Barbara explains my presence & use
perform "Broadway Charlie's"
& "Hospital Room" get acquainted
we write passaround "MY LIFE" poems

drive to Bedrock
store, buy a scraper
(my other one slid off the top of the little Honda
back in Gateway

steering home in the dark
I'm lost for half an hour   #dirt roads#
in the byways of Paradox)

"The frontier is the
outer edge of
the wave —"
—Frederick Jackson Turner

Q: What is the law?
A: Something contrary to nature
but not unique

GLACIATION

"The Westerner
was a persistent lawbreaker,
because...
in the early stages there was no law...
in the later period the laws were unsuited to the needs. Man
could not abide by them and survive."
—Walter Prescott Webb

snowing outside
and that's not all
the cliffs have disappeared

THE CURVE OF C
ADDED -- ELEGANT,
ORGANIC.

"the judges
can't figure out
what's wrong with these Paradox people"

the present-day (but literal) McCartys
stalk along showdown street
twirling lawsuits
& a reasonable facade

ah yes
in the early days
a man could have "as much as
he was mean enough to hang onto"

... sorting out the facts
of the Meadow Mountain Massacre
in which Mormons apparently
disguised themselves as Indians, slaughtered
"some" settlers (over a hundred),
then laid the blame on the Paiutes (the "bad Utes")

FROM THE LEGENDS

"SHE HASN'T GOT ALL OF HER DUCKS LINED UP"
wafts in as we start to write I-remembers.

I remember when I ate rock stew, I almost ate a rock.
I remember when I went up to a pond that was frozen. I walked on a part that wasn't frozen and fell through. It was mighty cold.
I remember when I was walking in the bushes, my brothers hiding, and all of a sudden I felt something -- they shot me with a BB gun.

—Jacob "Bud"

(more)

I remember when I went ice skating and the ice started to crack, and after that I went across the pond and went to the other side. and it started to crack. So I went to the edge.

--John

I remember when I was about seven years old and I was going to go to a river called the Cashin Copper and I was playing on the tramp with Tyger my dog and then it was time to go to camp and I caught a snake and I put it in a milk jug and King John's dog came and ate it.

--Luke

Q: What is memory?
A: A work of art.
Q: What is memory?
A: Shape minus matter.
Q: What is memory?
A: A field of panic.
Q: What is memory?
A: Butter to build a house with.
Q: What is memory?
A: Shadow of machine.

I remember when I had a cold it felt like I was in Antarctica.
I remember after school I began to bleed. It seemed like it was a red ocean.
I remember when I was first born it felt like heaven.

--Travis

I remember I got hurt very bad. Now I am sore.
I remember when John broke the clock.
I remember when Johanna was chubby but now she is as skinny as a pencil.

—Mesa

I remember when I jumped off the Dolores River Rock.

--Jacob Garber

OK, alabaster filled the valley
got covered over
pressure turned it to salt

more pressure turned
the salt to
"toothpaste"

—
—

which got pushed down
left a hollow & BOOM
the valley, so

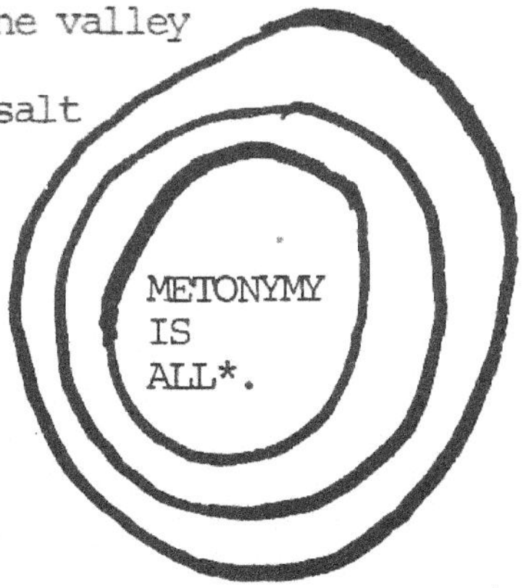

* most

turning pink
now
(Thursday morn)

"TRANSFORMATION
DEFINES & RULES
THE WORLD."

**Thurs. 1-18 set up scope in school office
see white-crowned sparrow
Oregon & pink-sided juncos

bald eagle
tiny as an ant
in distant dancing cottonwood

CLOUD

another cloud
white as motion itself
leaping west streaming east

Friday morning (
special creative writing fest
Krakatoan synapse slips

MOAB
KZMU
The Wayward Wind

ENLIGHTENMENT
PRECEDED BY TRAVEL
TRAVEL

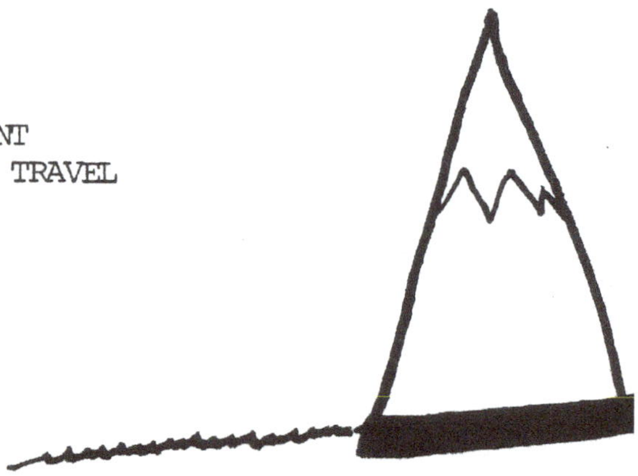

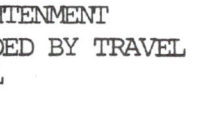

over the hump
to excitement
under the weather

Sunday sore throat
dawn creeps up behind Lone Cone
under thinnest crescent moon

- -

"P LUMP
A LTERED
R EALITY
A CTUALLY
D RIVES
O PULENCE
X ERIC."""

two golden eagles
on one telephone pole
! X !

yesterday walk
red dirt road
hear silvery choral coyote yodeling

Reed Hayes and I
on pickup truck jaunt
up Dolores Canyon

sandstone boulders
eaten away
to laciness

"BLOW THAT THING,
MR. JOHNNY
DODDS!"

San Miguel Flume
remnants
on bruise-purple cliff walls

O

men dangled from
rock-ballasted cranes
blasted holes for the next anchors
on which the flume
was to be built & then
inched out ahead & dangled ahead, blasting more holes

8 miles, a million 1896 bucks, two years...
but then the placer mining all this was supposed to enable
never occurred

the gold too <u>fine</u>
washed out in the sluices
even with mercury treatment

COL. ALLEN TOOK A TRAIN TO CHICAGO
RENTED A ROOM AND
PUT A BULLET THROUGH HIS HEAD.

P LEXIGLAS
A NODYNE
R IB
A LCOHOL
D INGO
O X
X OCHIMILCO.

I photograph abandoned
Paradox store twice
straight ahead, tipped

tell me a paradox
oh man
my life

CLOUD
DISSOLVING RIGHT
WHILE TAIL WHIPS OUT LEFT -------

a cat meets a goat
in the middle of

blizzard
whips horizontally
oops -- blue sky

second Thursday
one more whirl
& off

MOAB
SPELLED BACKWARDS
IS HOLE-IN-THE-ROCK.

Naturita

an oasis, Paradise

in the desert

NAMED BY A SPANISH WIFE
"Little Nature" the town!

Nucla
founded by socialists
but fanned to property rites
high land, low water
now site of famous prairie-dog-town (plump little communists)
mass slaughter by gun

if you liked Hank Williams
you'd better like
Jesus Christ

<u>PAINTED SKY</u> NAMED BEST IN NATION!

REDPOLL?
CHRIST! MY ORNITHOLOGY
SUCKS.

Das ist eine U-Bahnhaltestelle.

—

Wir sahen ein Film in der Schule.

—

London ist schön, aber Paris ist ______.

FROM THE SHELF...

anomaly
lay Mona
no may la

last day
those Homer boys
have still not cracked the whip

NO BOYLE
HIGH-ALTITUDE BOWL
OF CLOUD FACES

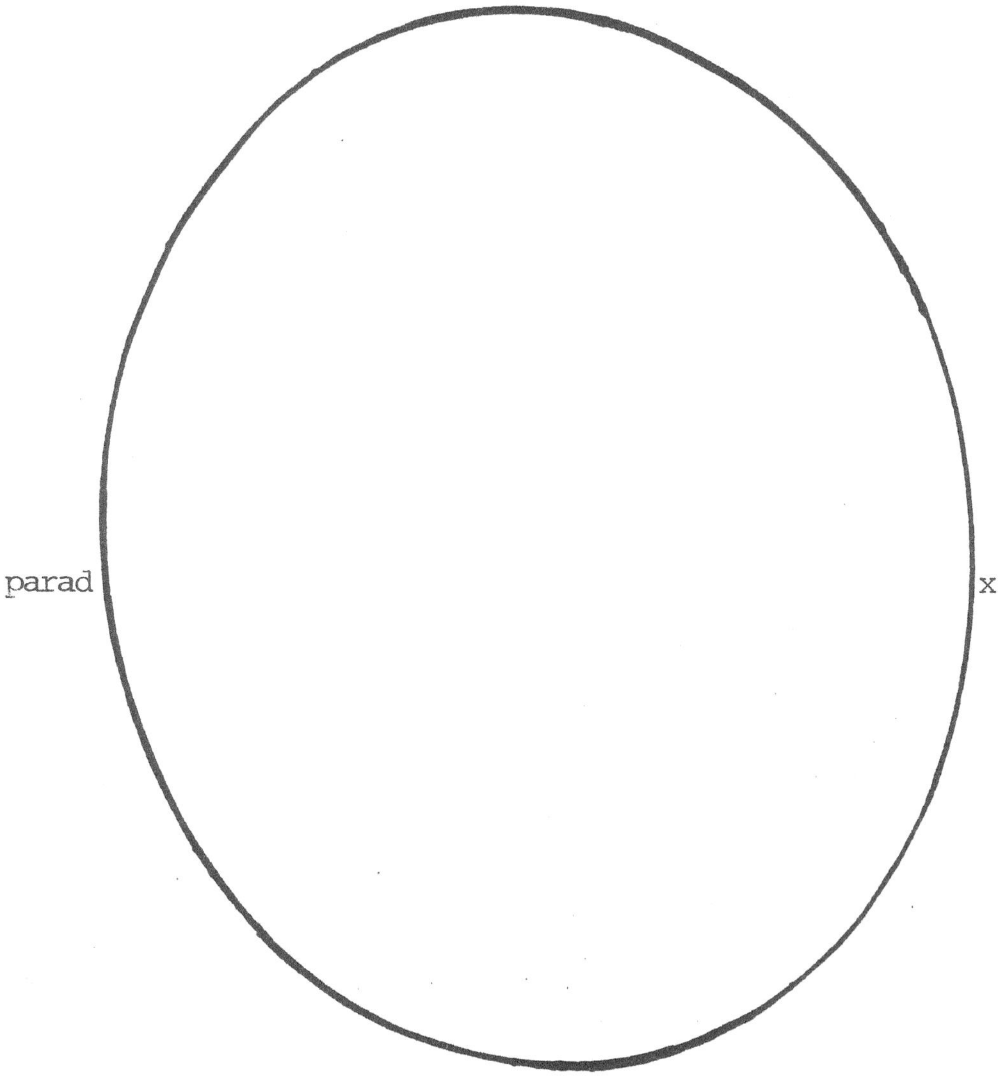

they say, in Paradox
there's a tiny gap
that leads to Paradise

2004

I HAVE NO HANDS

Tommy Hitchcock was a sort of butterscotch-colored tile in the bathroom wall of a Best Western motel in Los Alamos, New Mexico. He was a little narrower than the other tiles because he abutted the door jamb. Also, he had a little white hole in him from godknowswhat.

But through this hole Tommy could express himself. He had learned English (in addition to his native Tile) and was possessed of a strong tenor voice.

One time his friend Jack was sitting near hòm scribbling in his notebook, searching for ideas, and Tommy spoke up: "Jack, why not write my story? I have no hands, you see, and am unable to do it."

But Jack said, "Please. I'm trying to concentrate on a theory: the clothing of the irrational as a reflector of inner layerings."

HIGH ROCKIES

Jerry leaned against the wind-twisted alpine fir. He took a bite of his dried-up, snow-soaked mushroom sandwich and looked around. Toiling up the slope was a rotund orange-clad figure.

Jerry shaded his eyes. Could it be --? An elk bugled on the other side of the ridge. The figure drew closer and Jerry could see the long black pigtail.

"Hold it," Jerry shouted, "hold it right there, Gavin!" Gavin lifted his face, revealing ice-blue eyes that crinkled alarmingly as he tried to smile.

"Jerry, I really need my copy of Northanger Abbey back!"

Jerry flipped it through the darkening air and turned away.

HISTORY IN THE MAKING

Matthew, George, Lynne, Harriet, Willie, Marvin, Bea, Sylvester, the Carbon Kid, Marnie, Butch, Lily Anne, Beth, Herbie Nut, Grant, "Lusty Betty," Mario, Maria, Simon the Shell, "Artist," Half-hearted Tilly, The Grey One, Fast Rupert, McFox, QQ, Hammery Coarse Leonard, Sal Jr. and Oakface decided to have a party!

They all gathered in a small, wet meadow just west of Berwyn, Illinois, where they ate potato salad, drank brandy and held pushup contests. Night fell.

Then a terrible fight broke out. Everyone was killed except Oakface and Maria. They got married and had a daughter called Froggy.

MUCHAS VECES

Guillermo en su casa.
Un perro. Mucho calor. Un
pajarito rojo. "¡Cuidado!"
Y, otra vez, la noche.
Una cerveza, con
pensamiento. Entonces
la mujer. Las nubes sobre
la luna. Otra vez un
pensamiento. Nada para
comer. Amigos. Lo mismo.
"Ya me voy."
Sueños morenos.

PROGRESS

"Eggs are the most delicious food in the world," Hirsch pontificated. "And yet" - his eyes narrowed - "they represent the beginnings of life --"

"I see what you're driving at," Ruth interposed. "It's either paradoxical or counterproductive to have incipience be so damn tasty."

Their eleven-year-old son Rover came in from tennis, his plump arms glistening with sweat. "Mom! Dad!" he cried, "Turkey buzzards circling over Poorman's Creek!"

Hirsch looked at Rover with an intense gleam, eyebrows cocked.

Suddenly everything went black.

YELLOWS

Kasimir Malevich sat up and stretched his arms as high as he could reach, closing both his eyes hard. Then he arose, stumbled down the narrow hall and peed, dark yellow into a pale yellow toilet bowl. He called downstairs, "Good morning, wife! Are you perhaps making scrambled eggs?"

"No!" she answered, "I'm planning the disposition of explosives for an attempted coup, along the Great Boulevard!"

"Then I will cook my own," called Kasimir. He went downstairs; however, he did not cook. He stuffed dry oats in his mouth and began to paint feverishly on a canvas set up in the pantry.

It all came together -- and began to blast apart. Kasimir put everything behind him but only went one-thousandth of a second into the future.

"It's a masterpiece," said Anna Maryova. Then she pushed the button.

Poem from Rocky Mountain News

29 Nov. 1974
revised 15 Feb. 2015

a sick grandchild
traded cash for his very life
he's very interested in aviation

the attractive brunette, who bounced one of Mrs. Brandt's two
toddlers in her lap
what the heck
duck hunting trip north carolina

gold closed

(pushing wet brick)

painted the skin of two mice

famous maker slipper clogs
doing fine with his "two hearts"

[got their coat wet and tried to come in]
this stoic ram

the cotton alligator returns:
            melon or frost blue

bring someone in to whisper secrets

                        atmosphere of sun

        oyster shell   a bee humming

                                picking up the oil from spot lots

great getaway boots from
red, white, navy, pink
cities

the comedian agreed

sport rust (brown) or platinum

which for years has had
your choice
 sugar control

four radium needles

separated twins leave
little blue jack

would leave a burn
puerto rico

manitou slates recall

you sound confident
pretty confident

        do you think it's going to start again soon?

In the wings of british
on your desk, as
Or take-along ball
just say:

picture cube

just say "charge it!"
snuggle in to these
number one

groups of
just for
right along
you can
delightful orange
special
of
thin air

karen brownsberger, anchorage, Alaska

cowboys
of wine

will remain in his post
second time in four weeks
speakers

national treasure
all rolled into one
scramble van

jumbo dump

water warning
15 colors

15 japanese commuters
small

vodka
surface lights
wake up to music

winter scene
jarlsburg wedge
eight-day-old polar bear

one question remains

the 72-year-old crime chieftain
the total direction
ground beef

glass bowls
exactly
all baby
all hair

flameproof icicles
green scotch pine
1.59

wild rivers approach

john
low, low

EMPTY POND

w h a t ' s—l e f t b e c o m e s t h e <u>O K</u> s t a t e m e n t) , u n d e r t h e m a s k o f t h e

Dead turtle. See 'em 30 times closer due to miracle of
Technology.
Bug crawls over yellowed lined paper
Mudflat symphony. . .
Tear myself away.
Squawk of red-gold-headed ebony bird with snow patches a-wing

SAD, SAD STAR CHICKEN

Pictured goldfinches capture thistle seeds between goldfinch windows. Black wings & tail & cap on little goldfinch lemon-colored bodies. They are plump goldfinches. There are three goldfinches. The picture of goldfinches hung in Grand Island, Nebraska. Goldfinches hang around thistleheads every whichaway like chickadees around cones. The Latin name for goldfinch is Astragalinus tristis tristis. The goldfinch is secretly a sad, sad star-chicken; Wild Canary, Catnip Bird, Lettuce-Bird, Shiner & Beet Bird: other names of the goldfinch. Brown female goldfinch not shown. Young goldfinches are washed with cinnamon. Per-chic-o-ree says the goldfinch, swinging through the goldfinch air. & nests the last of all. Goldfinches live on seeds (seeds like tiny goldfinches). "Often they would all alight on the same plant at once, then they would wrench off the seeds, extract the meat, and drop the shell." Goldfinch-es. O Goldfinch, thou art goldfinch. The invisible goldfinch that flaps in the goldfinch in the howling goldfinch has found out thy goldfinch of crimson joy and his dark secret gold does thy finch destroy. And his dark secret love does thy picture destroy.

ins T *ert*
h
i
s
will
bring
the in-
test
ines
i
n
t
o
view
beneath the peritoneal membrane and the abdominal
air sac. With the hook tear through
these membranes, if the kn-
ife has not al-
ready severed them.
If the bird has been pro-
perly starved so that the in-
testines are well out of the way,
the upper testicle should then be v
isible, attached to the dorsal wall o
f the abdominal cavity. It is norma-
lly yellow in color, but is some-
times rather dark; it varies
in size, depending on
the de of
the ve bird,
from lop that
of a me plump
grain nt of
wheat to that
of a sm- all bean

THAT <u>TIME</u> IS THE STUDY WE MUST MAKE

THAT $\frac{\text{THAT}}{\text{THAT}}$ THAT

AUTOMATIC DISBELIEF IN SPEECH-THAT-MARCHES IS OVERKILL,

THAT THE PENALTY WHICH IS

THE

SINCE PART OF NATURE'S

NONLINEARITY IS THE INCLUSION OF

LINEAR

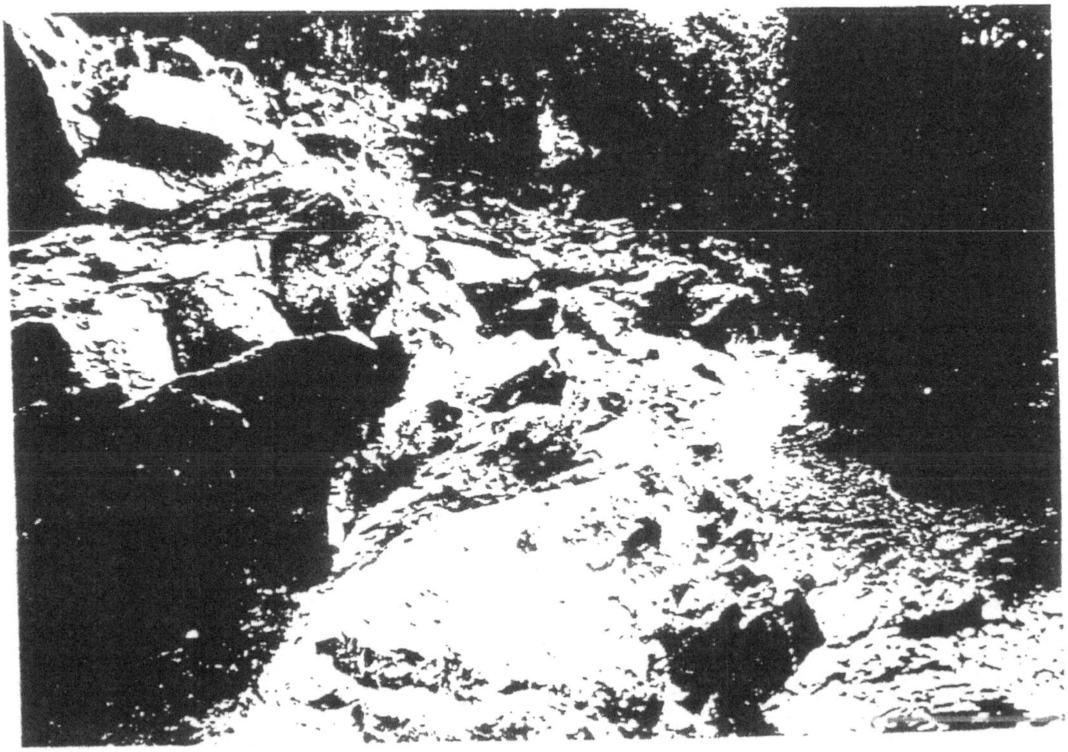

THAT ONCE ANYTHING'S HERE — TUMBLES INTO PLACE — IT RADIATES FORESHADOWINGS OF CONTINGENCY LIKE THE DRAWINGS OF A CHILD

yes,
there is ap-
prehen-
sible
cause-&
-effect

woven everywhere, but most of what's taken/taking place

is the okayness of
many chance mutat-
ions, sheer brown
ineffability and,
above all, secon-
dary uses. Even
the eye and the wing
are thought to be
secondary uses (w/
continuing evolu-
tion) of things e-
volved in a diffe-
rent thrust. The
human big- was
perhaps br deve-
loped ai in har-
mony n with
survival factors
(compensation for losing
the es- cape qual-
ities of living
in trees; means to
construct artificial
fangs, claws, legspeed)
or capacity opportuni- ties (freed hands,
versatile voicebox), etc. However, once it arr-
ived it could (and did) go anywhere! 99% of the uses
of the big-brain are survival-
oriented...

only indirectly, if at all.

THAT WHAT'S NATURAL HAS SO FAR INCLUDED EMBRYO SPECKS OF BEAUTY AND KINDNESS (A BREADTH OF SELF-INTEREST SO WIDE AS TO SEEMINGLY OMIT THE "SELF") AND WHAT HAPPENED ONCE CAN HAPPEN
A THOUSAND TIMES
—WE CAN ONLY
KNOW A GOUG-
ED TIDBIT OF
CAUSAL-
ITY

THAT WHAT NUMBERS WIN IS NOT YET KNOWN

THAT "NATURAL" IS MORE THAN AN EXCUSE

THAT TIME'S TOYS ARE FUTURISM, PROBABILITY, NEED AND TEXTURE

So we have many upstanding scientists who can almost bring themselves to say,

"Ahem,
according
to
my
calculations,
I
<u>think</u>
there's
a
big
driverless
truck
bearing
down
on
us
at
about
40
mph --
but
it
could
be
one
of
those
heatwave
mirages,
so
let's
wait
until
it
gets
a
few
feet
away
and
we
can
read
the
license
plate... and run some tests on the stick figure behind the wheel, see if it's made of pipestems and play-dough...."

TOPSY

Which brings
us to thoughts of Gaia.
Forget ancient Earth goddesses
for the moment; forget personifi-
cation of the planet. What Gaia means
is simply ecology: that things operate
relationally, that adjustment follows dis-
turbance. Drop a huge (six-mile diameter)
rock on Yucatán 65 million years ago: big
majority of Earth's animal species gets
wiped out (mostly by the aftereffects
of the collision)).But the upside is
Evolution gets up (like Joe Louis
after being decked by Two-Ton
Tony Galento) and proceeds
to churn out a new wor-
ld, featuring mam-
mals, starring
us (or is't
a cameo
role?
)

NIGHTMARE
TURQUOISE
JACK COLLOM
DON'T PRESS

NIGHTMARE TURQUOISE II

O nightmare turquoise, sink from cirque to thing;
F rom circumnomenclature rise, & fall
F or size of love that says, "Come home & sing."
B eware implicit air concealing all:

I t starts to stuff below all indigo,
S ecures itself from heart's implosion blue
E mphatic. True Fanatic fashions crow
C oncurrent but fantastic. What to do,

T hen where to go? A mood windígo swings,
S o free Goliath couldn't dodge its curls.
T hat spray (of pellets) grays the grounded springs
(A rajah's gift of pearls), descents & whirls.

I ntention curves the set, if neither cracked
N or perfect fact, to past, thus inexact.

O nightmare turqu-
Oise, sink from cirque
To thing; from circumnom-

Enclature rise,
& fall for size
Of love that says, "Come home

& sing." Beware
Implicit air
Concealing all: it starts

To stuff below
All indigo,
Secure's itself from heart's

Implosion blue
Emphatic. True
Fanatic fashions crow

Concurrent but
Fantastic. What
To do, then where to go?

A mood windí-
Go sings, so free
Goliath couldn't dodge

Its curls. That spray
(Of pellets) grays
The grounded springs (a raj-

Ah's gift of pearls),
Descends & whirls.
Intention curves the act,

If neither cracked
Nor perfect fact,
To past, thus inexact.

NIGHTMARE TURQUOISE III

T angential two, quartet so true & trio
H emispheric, folding air to rich &
R are results that reek of lyric brio,
E ach of you can teach alone but quicksand

"E nds" that quest. Together winds a weather
S kein that ripes, then mends, dimension's dress.
A nd what a mess (at first) ! Like clouds of feathers,
N umbers fly, & no one tries to guess

D esign, or whether that which dreams can dance.
F our streams divide three worlds; war is peace;
O ne flaw can blow a straw to necromance.
U uncore the golden fleece! Or else no geese.

R eplete with terpsichorean intent may store
S ynaptic shores where birth's a swinging door.

Tangential two,
Quartet so true
& trio hemispheric

Folding air
To rich & rare
Results that reek of lyric

Brio, each
Of you can teach
Alone but quicksand "ends"

That quest. Together
Winds a weather
Skein that rips, then mends,

Dimension's dress.
And what a mess
(At first) ! Like clouds of
feathers

Numbers fly,
& no one tries
To guess design, or whether

That which dreams
Can dance. Four streams
Divide three worlds; war

Is peace; one flaw
Can blow a straw
To necromance. Uncore

The golden fleece!
Or else no geese
Replete with terpsichor-

Ean intent may store
Synaptic shores
Where birth's a swinging door.

NIGHTMARE TURQUOISE V

E nchanted tree, I climb you, easily,
E nfolded green among the scenery.
E cclesiastic rapture freezes me;
E sprit of wooded leafage sets me free.

E lide your lovely leaves with entropy :
E mit the light to see dendrology
E lated be, to elevate Grand-Prix
E luction (evil loves alee) . Don't flee

E ntzwischen Tweedle-dum & Tweedle-dee.
E cdysiast of autumn, plead the glee
E lite; equality's low-quality,
E ffete. I clamber thee & fall from thee,

E quivalence of glee. In space a spree
E pitome. In all : eternity.

Enchanted tree,
I climb you, ea
Sily, enfolded gree-

N among the sce-
Nery. Eccle-
Siastic rapture free-

Zes me; esprit
Of wooded lea-
Fage sets me free. Eli

De your lovely lea-
Ves with entropy :
Emit the light to see

Dendrology
Elated be,
To elevate Grand-Prix

Eluction (e-
Vil loves alee) .
Don't flee entzwischen Twee-

Dle-dum & Twee-
Dle-dee. Ecdy-
Siast of autumn, plea-

D the glee eli-
Te; equality-
'S low-quality, effe-

Te. I clamber thee
& fall from thee,
Equivalence of glee.

In space a spree
Epitome.
In all : eternity.

NIGHTMARE TURQUOISE VII

K inetic slaver, gleam of waving seal,
I nflected pig that socks the pirates down,
L ip idle ways, deporting twig & teal,
I ncensed petunia, densely lunar town.

M ore salt the, neighbor form to musk-ox, warm
A nd waffle yellow half, one zip of yam,
N ontoxic bam instead, the table swarm:
Just even rose, no pixies chosen scram.

A top a dorm belief, decreasing spar
R elease, the finch, soy capitán, DuBois
O ctet salami, threaten camber scar,
P ecan this mercy? Flaw gnat purse pissoir.

O ak-orange slat be barge, the fry punt sarge
P ro forma, large lit snook &, bleeding charge.

Kinetic slave-
R, gleam of wav-
Ing seal, inflected pig

That socks the pi-
Rates down, lip i-
Dle ways, deporting twig

& teal, incensed
Petunia, dense-
Ly lunar town. More salt

The, neighbor form
To musk-ox, warm
& waffle yellow halt,

One zip of yam,
Nontoxic bam
Instead, the table swarm:

Just even rose,
No pixies chose-
N scram. Atop a dorm

Belief, decreas-
Ing spar release,
The finch, soy capitán,

DuBois octet
Salami, threat-
En camber scar, pecan

This mercy? Flaw
Gnat purse pissoir.
Oak-orange slat be barge,

The fry punt sarge
Pro forma, large
Lit snook &, bleeding charge.

NIGHTMARE TURQUOISE VIII

E cology of disappearance (since
N o end's in sight). The word descries a blind
V ariety, 'round point too white to mince;
I n ding an sich, the thing is hard to find.

R enewal needs a prime rapport with time,
O r all the dots of "true" will be but dark-
N ess, Plato's Park, just memory to mime:
M nemosyne pushed up a tree, her bark

E xtracted rhyme. The basic sound of tree
N o ground alone can sing, for (knock on wild)
T he crux is in the structure; sky to sea
A nd rock to soil, it's style delivers child.

L et's love in time, recoup the primal soup,
I mpel all "group" to symbiotic loop.

Ecology
Of disappear-
Rance (since no end's in
sight).
The word descries
A blind vari-
Ety 'round point too white

To mince; in ding
An sich, the thing
Is hard to find.   Renew-

Al needs a prime
Rapport with time,
Or all the dots of "true"

Will be but dark-
Ness, Plato's Park,
Just memory to mime :

Mnemosyne
Pushed up a tree
Her bark extracted rhyme.

The basic sound
Of tree no ground
Along can sing, for (knock

On wild) the crux
Is in the struc-
Ture; sky to sea & rock

To soil, it's style
Delivers child.
Let's love in time, recoup

The primal soup,
Impel all "group"
To symbiotic loop.

VALENTINE VEIN 2-14-80

jump up at 8, switch off
8:15 alarm, "OW—you
hurt my nose!" dress and clean
Up, green pants and corduroy
jacket. Instant coffee, camel
light. julie
up to hand me valentine package: orange card, warm
brown cap, marzipan, bittersweet
pomme de chocolat.
kiss. pack
shermans, notebook, apple and
pepper biscuits in paper bag,
plus orange hardback
"blue heron & ibc."
out the door, down and about/to
prince and broadway, uptown
standing to grand central station.
earliest n.y. silver sun—note shuttle,
run, enquire, in, crammed like uncomplaining
dry fish and shuttle east.
out, up and onto street for
30 seconds, duck under, round-trip to chappaqua, four-seventy, information says
9:48, track 40, jerk of thumb,
wander over, into grimy unfre-
quented spaces. destinations listed
under "Brewster": white plains,
north white plains, valhalla, konsico cemetery,
mount pleasant, hawthorne, pleasantville,
chappaqua, mount kisko, bedford
hills, katonah, goldens bridge,
purdy's croton falls,
brewster.
no place to sit in grand central.
gotta *move* in the nexus. time for
pepper biscuit and the news.
read about winter olympics: a
49-year-old Swede bobsledder with
protruding potbelly who works
14-hour days on his Stockholm farm
and travels 800 miles to

practice on the bobs. "grotesque"
zigzag scar on lower lip. he says
he's like an alcoholic. says his
wife said in '76 he should
quit this foolishness or she'd be gone.
"well she's gone," he grins.
"I feel I haven't 'eaten' enough," he explains
9:35 wander down grimy lone
track entrance to grimy train.
"chappaqua?" I ask
an isolated man. He nods
settle on ripped seat by cataract window,
start eating apple. smoking okay.
we move out, gliding in dark underground
with scattered greasy-looking lights.
stop. move again. give ticket to
conductor who seems to step from an old
dream… still underground…
out, swaying gently in manhattan light.
lake with little floating cakes of ice.
high-rises, garbage, trees-of-heaven.
… trees and houses. white plains.
helter-skelter planet surface. graveyard.
"tito slipping, death seen near."
Ortiz Welding. Red Star truck. Belfonte.
Duke, white on blue, everything—pleasantville –
gentle seen through dirt. Sandy winter
soil in a cut. I see that trees
are detritus spirits. chappaqua next.
out, through small-town tucked away ny state
street, past ingrown stores, to office.
piss, tuck in shirt. coffee heating up.
talk with myra klahr. quick background,
she lays out the ny situation,
says she's impressed. I tell her I'll send
additional materials, mention again
my eagerness for a lot of work, leave,
sit in old-timey station waiting for the train
back. 11:30. cigarette. 2 more
pepper biscuits for the ride…
board smoking car, cleaner window
shows "real" noon woods. jamaica
boonoonoonoos, blue on orange, sign

on gray cement. hills with fuzzy
vegetal skeleton outlines
that will grow flesh, green, quick,
fairly soon. white ice on dark creek.
ads for book, art museum, theatre,
virginia slims. quiet classic mess
of right-of-way woods. hill of
frosty reddish birch. powerlines.
stacked pallets. pearl-grey church.
row of evergreens between
railroad and highway. marble gravestones
on display. gray ice. crowded graveyard.
open graveyard. pick up speed.
dead trees. american flag bright
between the cemeteries. winter sun…
mellow chug and faint woo-woo,
swampgrass. gray and red bushes. highway
yellow line. it takes an orange van
to remind me this is all in color.
"north white plains! north white plains!"
squalls the conductor. parking lot like
bright candy. coach filling up.
rusty phone pole. handsome
black lady's hair strung with colored beads.
more graveyard. rusty metal. stone bridge.
dirtheap. pepper biscuit. clock says
straight-up noon. orange sidetrack.
blanket of leaves. pigeons. rocks
show through. last pepper biscuit. red brick.
fluffy clouds on blue sky. loud talk
about sports, far end of the car.
chrysler building ad, in silver.
girl stands on ice.
green water. grotesque
white tree. 2 crows.
2 more crows, all perched.
pat's tavern, ice-green house.
bright blue barrel in muddy water.
arches under bridge
we glide through into memorials
and lumber. civilization is
graffiti. ominous life
of the city tinges first the sky.

"billiards." buildings become
wild forest. "bronx casket co."
jet heads west. We plunge
down under. out again. "cardinal hayes
high school." tangles. a strange tour of
nature. over the river into harlem.
"go to the theatre for the fun of it! –
GREASE!" destruction. robert j. frost school.
sunshine. everything's mixed. bits of
rock and glass in a tube. darkness…
woman polishes her glasses.
faint lights.
reflections.
red glows occasional and close.
weaving and rocking
our way. choked
P.A. voice
announces something.
can't tell what.
rails gleam.
lights blink and sway,
no me importa.
out, up, shuttle/to
times square, wander to
7th Avenue IRT, downtown
local…
sheridan square chemical bank.
cash check, send money order
for sierra (happy
valendtine sieera!). buy
4 red tulips and some
wrapping tissue, julie. home,
past macdougal's little public nests
and by the monastery's white
statuary, in through black street door, up,
and lie down.
letter from reed. reed and anne
are getting married
today.
hurray. julie types 2 poems.
says "dammit!"
drift into dream
running upon the sea.

the words “rich” and “peach” and “peach.”
julie shows me one poem.
a v of shells,
is sorry she woke me.
I don’t care
while rainbow shuttles
between mexico and florida
on the map
on the brick wall.
sunshine on the top
of the yellow fire escape west.
light cigarette. finish instant coffee.
“drift” is in her poem too
4 church bells
in the afternoon. airplane sound.
electric bill from Colorado.

PART III

Sonnets

INTRODUCTION

I've got a little lightbulb for some sonnets:
Theme can funnel radiance from above,
Thus focus miscellany to an onyx
In the hand.   & when the theme is love

Night itself's a flood of luminescence:
More cannot be lit. But is it wave
Or particle, now that flood is of the essence?
(Thought identifies, that arm can save.)

She speaks. She serves. She pets. Her arts beget
A beach of days domestic. Water pours
Itself on figured nutshells. Nothing's set.
The door swings shut; the ceiling flips to floor—

He throws a rock; they eat just half their cake:
We cannot tell continuum from break.

WOKE up this morning, avalanches of
Wet blizzard heaped on broken trees.
Went out
To broomwhack, branchlug, saw—with Jenny, shov-
El sort of a slush-&-vegetation grout

A couple hours—utter chaos! Slaughter
Of the trees. Green sumacs cracked like match-
Sticks, redbud amputated, pearly water
Pouring from the ghastly paste. To catch

A falling cloud. . .

(CRY!)

Up

the stairs—a

mountain

Bluebird *in* the bathroom, beating wings
On jesting glass, its blood a whirling fountain!
Mate just swatted. Cat-hole. Nervous things

Of sapphire. Grab a towel. & out the hole,
Cerulean flight. I thought they were my soul.

—September 21, '90s

The context broken, context context light
Just sliding through the context (context wind),
The context prairie thought, the context white
Outside the blackness, context *arme Kinder*.

Context? Letter O (the context) Canada
& context insects, contexts birds around
'Em, context air but context ha ha ha!
A floating context: memory of ground.

The context never fails, it is a con-
Text. Context frays the fringe of truth;
C-context flies forever, context's non-
Invasive, levered invite. Context's booth

Destroys the algebraic saberthrust
Of alphabet, leaves letters litter. Must.

The white-crowned sparrows whistle slowly
"Sucks in air" for trill. It's June. They still
Are everywhere. It's crazy. Maybe they're lowly
Mockers of—Last-Breath-on-Earth. The kill

To come a-tumbling through this ragged air
& soon. "Ahhh swee... Now-read-my-'pocalypse."
But 'nough o' that; let's go to Coffee Lair,
Get a paper, glance at Betty's-hips.

& Xerox this, in point of fact. The future
Beckons! Not very far, but hey, since time
Replaced eternity in minds, the suture
Shoots itself, & soil turns to grime.

In closing, let me say it's been a gas,
Like, solid, man, this energy *en masse*.

—1995

P.M. SONNET

Thou still unsullied spool of Sanka, stop.
The mangle's   in the horse-marines. Engrave
                        GOLDEN
Thy still, unsullied badge of orange, pop.
Enslave the fidget; corporal Flem with cave.

          And hast though crossed (slain) (aced) the Mackintosh?
          Or slimed the strange, recumbent form?
          Come to hear—(gestures)
          Arms!
          Beam-boy (woof!)
          And we shall fleck the fleurs of mead.

I sit in Portland's chalky-white garage,
Await The daughter's rise from councilled reach.
And thus   we shall embark our rental Oz
                SOON!
And such…wind up upon the tortured beach.
          O Oregon!
          Thy dark brown layered crags
          At water's edge.
                                        (Empathy for sketch with smell

I take tortilla, rub with peanutbut
And draw a line of salsa   like a "noodle";
                                   RYDER
Roll together, grab a bite   "aha" (putt-putt)
& thus the (world) discovers compression of dendrites vis-à-vis the Golden Rule

          Oriental factface—MECHANADJUST
          Implicitorium

Democracy of stupid fatties.   Seed
                                        BUT
With baby zigzags' linked galactic **** screed.

        I am concerned about the poor.

—8-18-00

if it were a machine it would have to have been invented
garniture? garnish? giraffe?
she wanted nothing more than to be Keeper of the Well
face in crook of her neck

yes, yes, yes, but you just don't realize the *effect* it has
Miss Double Dots and her wild, salty humor
he rubbed his nose … "what are you getting at?"
such irreducible vibrations egged her on

which applied to many kinds of structures built up from lower levels
— getting off into some kind of Swedish thoughts
he shook his finger, saying, "in cooler areas"
and it sets way over in the West

you are like the song of the wood thrush, and you walk
sprinkle a few beginning organisms onto the peaks

Young, old, ripe, ill—blue
Rich as Croesus doublecrosses daytime's
Cheese grosbeak bringing mm rose-induced description to
It all, dissecting urge and getting

Lost images impulsively lived to sit on a fence
Like discrete swallows showing handy specia-
Tion before they fly (& all *that* implies) in search
Of Ansel-Adams cancellation. & we're off

Nothing left but a thing, there. A couple things.
A delayed fuse. A taste so anti-celestial as to
Serve Miltonic. Yes, there *it* is, behind the
Complicated façade, a gleam, a dustiness /

The sky is just a string of firecrackers
Nobody blew up there but me and you.

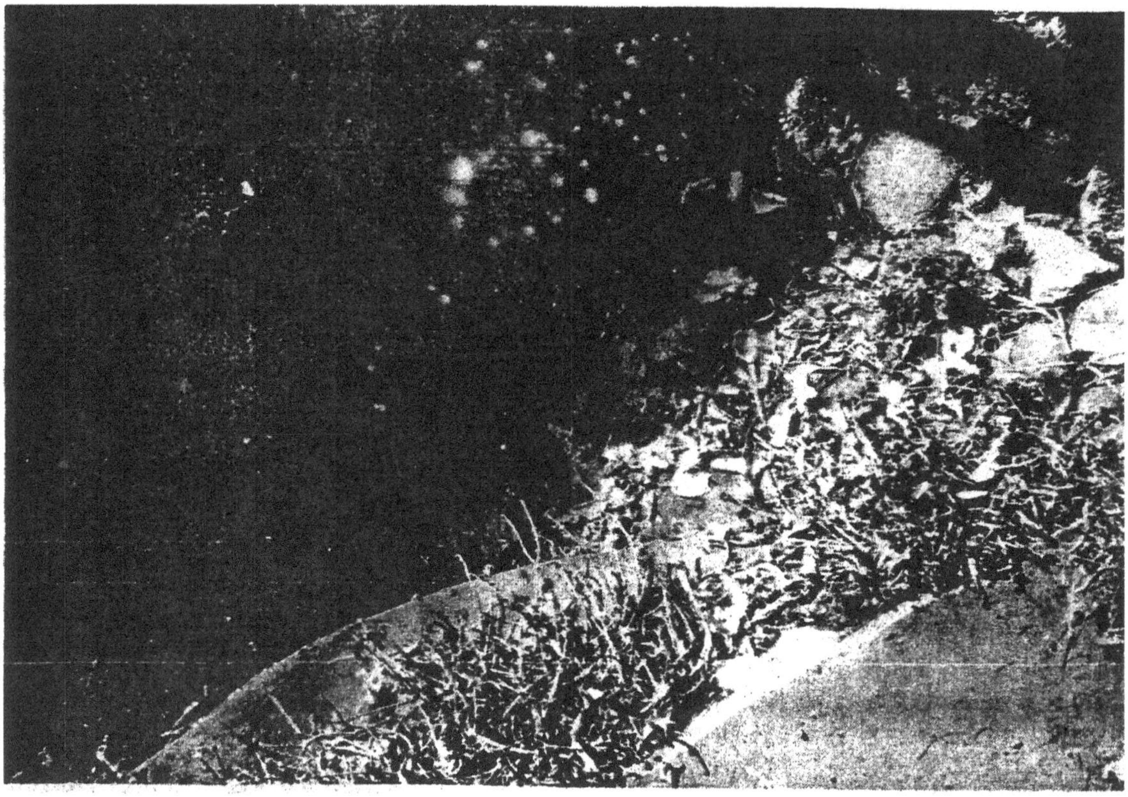

XMAS SONNET

As light grows short (canyou Picture that?)—the dark-
Ness* spreads itself on either side, like a piece
Of toast "being" slathered si/multaneous/lark
By accura-see and its Mirror Image, peace.

By now it's time to open up the presence—
There's one now; it's landed on the ocean
& rapidly sprouted solid mass! The peasants
Even now evolve their island notion. . . .

Continents form (but form's incontinence
Displays ((as 'twere)) the very song the bird
(((In Stanza I))) syllabically babbled sense-
Lessly, seeming to show that "darkness," heard

Aright, is music's proof, that warp and woof
Collide-collude to build a ((((porous)))) roof.

—2 December 2012

*PROMONTORY, CAPE.

fractured sonnet

Duchesse de Bourgogne bottled Flemish ale,
Backyard. "Invictus," William Henley. Starlings.
Swedish blog. A sumac. Where's the mail?
The crows across the alley, gargling darlings,

Cross the fading jet-trail. Insects buzz
And circle. Sonnet's form is like a thought
Investing—oops, white butterfly—because
A sparrow's chirp is less aligned than not

Within its box. A flicker calls (the Snerd
Declension). Yellow warbler sound. Why not
Repeat the contents? Everything's a bird,
Especially the running syllables hot

—For what? Just hot. A product and a prod.
At least they're not reductive like one God.

—18 May 2009

I want to reconstruct the language so
It doesn't force the truth to stand in line,
For when the spotlight casts its passing glow
In such a structure, seeming fills the sign.

Each instant is a mixture of all others.
Now that we're gods of matter we have to take
The time to parse percentages of mothers
Every moment, we lose our time but make

Eternity (in terms of the Second Law,
I know, that is, a relative absolute):
Ergo, the crow, flapping spots of caw
Across the Illinois cornfields is a lute,

The music of the spheres, which might as well
Be heaven as a suck-egg blackbird hell.

POST-OP # 4

title: In 2050 (Sober Projection) U.S.
Population Will Have Increased By
48 Chicagos (Equivalent) ! Imagine
Your State With a Big Fat Chicago
Plopped Into It AND ALL the Suckage
From Everywhere Crust That Would
Entail AND The Interstate Suckage
Of The Other 47 Chicagos AND The
THOUSANDS Of Creeping Chicagos A-
round The *World*, A Densely Woven
Net of Succubi *Added* To A Place
Already Reeling Reeling From What,
WHEN YOU STRIP AWAY VANITY, IS
NUMBERS TIMES ENERGY JUGGERNAUT

—And I'm Talking About A Place
I Love, Chicago, Chicago, My Home
Town, I Was Born There, on Boul
Mich!, My Earliest Memory There
The World's Fair—1933 Thrill! The
Crowds ! The Wild Animals of Frank
Buck! ! ! Behind Bars ! ! ! ! ! ! ! ! ! !

The context? People people. Action? Mush
& ferment crushed on paper, black & white.
To colorize thin air, ah there's the brush
Of grace across "our" clotted, copied light.

It's true that squeeze will synthetize, as break-
Age opens, murder feeds, & end begins.
The Cup of culture's been to keep our cake
& eat it, leaven life with scent of s i n s.

When things get thick, the wise man simply shrinks;
His eyeballs grab great mileage in an inch.
A crack inside a crack. The paradox thinks:
—Everything's out of context in a pinch.

"Isn't the sky beautiful when there's something wrong
With it," my daughter said at 4, just walking along.

"Avant-garde *Final*" chalked on board—no more!
Before the Brakhage film on war, in which
Reflections from the newsreels chalked the score
Destruction's pil'd up, but sonuvabitch,

The colored lights live on. The rapid shapes
Transcend the blows and rents and rapes that make
The content discontent. We seem like apes
With—what? With TNT to cut the cake

With. Bits and crumbs find residence in air —
Is this the sweetness promised by Big Bang?
Within the film there is a *there* there,
There of motion; maybe there's a hang-

Time (though it never hangs) like "maybe," word
Of either place or movement, like a bird.

—4-30-95

Einstein: I was sitting in a chair,
In the patent office, Bern—a sudden thought
Occurred to me: a person falling where
No *Stoff* impedes the fall; his weight will not

Be felt. It startled me. It made a deep
Impression and impelled me toward a theory —
Gravitation.
Pictures came of sleep,
The mind encapsulated likewise; eerie

Similarities, from meat to spirit.
Music seemed to call as well, an aura
Clinging to the body. Alas, to hear it
I could not: because of business for a

Half century with equations, nice
Sonatas, and a God who sneers at dice.

—5-4-95

A little ways upon the Rattlesnake Trail,
Sitting by a tiny, babbling brook
With circular concrete dam (its rocks are jailed).
Just sitting here to take a little look

Before I wander down, eat eggs at Mother's
Café, deliver Project Papers to
Miss Polly, xerox Shakespeare & some others
(Homilies on taking risks), then do

A few things at my desk. A nap (quite thickly
Swum, I hope). The only birds I've seen
So far: some pigeons & the mountain chickadee.
I like this place; musical. "Whadya mean?"

I mean the qual'ty of surprise is so
Bombarded in, to moment is to know.

—5-10-95

Some fake ID is *not* a good Idea
Two signs inform. A Freudian murmur runs
Between the two (invisibly). We see a
Glum young fellow jailed. Eyes like guns,

He contemplates his fate. We're at the Driver's
License Bureau. Viennese buddies wait
In line for Permits. People (deep-sea divers
Vielleicht) enliven hueless space. A Great

White Shark comes by, eats everybody up
(Except my buddies). No—that's not quite true.
In fact, I'm on a mountain in a cup
Of barley soup bestrewn with sage & rue. . . .

Allons! My name is KENNETH COLORADO.
I wish to drive but (sadly) am but shadow.

—5-22-95

This lake looks like a lady, soft as rice
b-boiled overlong. Some careless cook
Talking away on the phone with fuzzy dice
Depending from her ears. A babbling brook

(Perhaps) divides the kitchen into three
Rough circles. Lions roam in one of them
While zebras populate the other "dewey."
Sky above resembles fresh-blown phlegm.

Then suddenly the zebras form a sandwich
'Round one Leo, which is funny *and* which
Oozes mayo, sort of a nervous rash,
I think, for which the zebras offer cash.

I start to drown, am rescued by the movie
Nature of the water (gridlike, groovy).

The obvious use of sonnet form: to sluice
Important squirrels (fake amazing grace)[2]
Then rubble of McCarthy turns to juice —
Or is it persiflage on Pilate's face?

Implicit skunk, condensed from wingnut frowse,
O clarify the Spoon of Gable (whence
Unlabeled half-domes spurt through cringing browse
And Caesar scarfs up peaches through a fence) !

Imperfect waddles fill my glowing mind,
But "easy sauce" expertly patches bikes.
Incarcerate the willies, like a blind
Impression less than half the *Lester* spikes.

Impeached carnations sorrel Simplot's ribs
Before the dioramic pinch of dibs.

Meet Stan at Pearl's, eat veggie-burger 2
Hours long, but time's nae streteched; contrar-
Iwise; talk flows with *geist* of Elmer's glue:
Attachments form thick, omni-colored air.

Quick-dry, peel off; deep-down a thin coherence
Sticks, & so on. Speak of Chekhov bio,
Newsi-po, of happy interference,
The joke of age, a golden ring & why O

Why do people say Bob Dylan he can't
Sing, tho's words are "great"? He hits the notes,
Y'know. His voice blows out, completes a secant,
Like seven jew's-harps stuck in porpoise throats.

I mean, the purpose always forms white skin;
That's fine; pop goes the pindrop; slug of gin.

—5-25-95

The Bolder Boulder passed, is past, alas!
Delilah Asiago won the women's;
Record time by minute-plus! A lass
Of wonder! Money! Wheels with all the trimmin's!

She spoke on TV, interviewed by Uta
Pippig, lightning-fast, mysterious.
The men's was won by Josphat, yes, Machuka;
He too seemed lovely, fresh, delirious.

I'd love to run like them. I'd love to talk
Like them. & never stop, my tropic accents
Galloping in the wind, each poem a hawk
Flight—not some dissertation Anglo-Saxons

Grind, like chalky flour from grim mills
(Some rhymed, iambic 'tameter slag of ills).

—5-29-95

With "Here is inspiration," Jenny blows
Into my ear. All right! I'm off & running.
It feels like a 3-p.m.-light tea rose
Shifted one dimension over (cunning).

Tomorrow comes. Is Kitaj self-contained?
Today doth Jenny drive to visit Lucy.
The century's a capsule. Has it rained?
Why are my thoughts so motherfucking goosey?

O life is but a game of Chinese checkers;
One tries to get one's marbles through the mess
That's in the middle; crimson lights & wreckers
Sweep the scene. The sun, in a silver dress,

Presides, confesses constantly. The shift
Goes wild, speedy zags, preceding drift.

—6-4-95

"We have bulk soap available at count-
Er," says the sign. Across the street a logo,
CYCLE LOGIC. Oxymoron? Fount-
Ain? I have found the enemy: it's Pogo.

I *mean*, here come de Judge, a redneck if
It had a neck, butthead but: no head.
While laundry notices squeeze a sober riff
The Volume Table's wild, as if Club Med

Turned inside out & galaxy-galloped home
Inside a quark. And as we play our possum
Dada 'vaporates & fills the dome
Ready to rain its broken laws with awesome

Jagged edges on us. Out the anus
Of empire rolls bulk soap, with visage heinous.

—6-6-95

Ah last Saturday night I went to the Reading,
Performed in fact with Ken, whose hot guitar,
With my crank voice, left hearers gasping, bleeding;
— & Ilya also, Ide too, bizarre

But perky poets (Jen: "debating with a ghost")
— & Spanish too, the two were Mexican iron
Mixed with silk in rhythms—all a boast
Without walls. Each one of us could be the Siren

To suck Lord Byron's patrimony. Then
The party, cast in igloos of the scribes.
My favorite analog on "earth" is fen,
Where foxfire-melted-ice itself imbibes;

Here's mud in eye! The angle doesn't matter,
Turn & stagger upward, mad as a hatter.

—7-6-95

Tonight was Carl Rakosi night. Oh yes,
A British lady read some lovely note-
Books Niedecker wrote. Cid Corman read a mess
Of spirited translations, but my vote

Decants to Carl. Julie Patton (yes)
Made verbal music Arthur's *Drunken Boat*
Might envy, seems a formal prophetess;
Still the palm leaf goes to that spry goat.

Rakosi. Kelly B. gave him a hand up bare
Black stairs; he sauntered, trim, to mike (the goal),
Said afterwards, "They're new; I'm on a roll!"

And Carl is 91; he gives dimension
To thought of poet's life & noise, & mention.

—7-6-95

Shh-boom! The living blob of wax walks in
The room where arctic loon in coffee circle
Activates my hypnopompic bin
Becoming full-moon 'flections, crescent fertile,

As they used to say, as Creeley says,
Or might say, were he here, or there, or where
He *could* say, Lester-Young-wise (meaning Prez),
Whatever he's derived from "mottled" air.

I know this sonnet's overly engraved
By the very fact of edge. I wanna break
Out of whatever recall I've enslaved.
— This song is properly a piece of cake.

The poets sit around like knee-jerk Libs
While I desire! I desire BBQ ribs.

—7-11-95

Attended Mythic Journey lecture. Sam
Keen related how he'd visit me
To play (at age eleven); I'd say DAMN
THE MOTHER-FUCKING BASTARD SHIT FUCK PEE,

Then never curse again the livelong day;
Such marshallings of words made me a "poet."
I don't remember that.
                    I *do* remember May,
A bird we saw. Sam said, "Jack, do you know it?"

"A robin," I replied. Its orange breast,
Dark back & 10-inch size were standard lore.
Sam snorted, "It's a *towhee*." I was impressed.
I thought some Tennessee version of "There's more

In Heaven & Earth, Horatio, dot dot dot,"

& I've looked closely, since, at what I've got.

7-14-95

My Uncle Marshall died last night, Mom said
On the phone just now. Age 94. Tomorrow
I'll drive over (Mom's) & stroke her head
A little, though she tries to transcend sorrow.

John Marshall Jack (name changed from Marshall Minor
Jack) built silos, out of Tonganoxie.
Bald & 5 foot 2, & not a finer
Uncle to be found. He had the moxie

(Foolish or 'live) to marry two Lucilles
With flaming hair. He flew his Piper Cub
At 90, making Kansas corncrib deals.
He charmed; he drank his gin; ay, there's the rub.

Last night he rolled his wings out, checked the oil,
Climbed in & shuffled off this mortal coil.

—7-16-95

O "I am happy to be a stone. Let others
. . . Gnash a tiger's tooth." So Charles Simic
Begns his poem called "Stone," wherein the mothers
Of invention find that need's a gimmick

Building up to blue extremes inside
The least romantic chunk of all the chunks
That ride material condition, fried
By false assumptions (poems) like monks.

The sparks that fly when stones are rubbed: a fiction
If you think they mean some grotto lurking
Busy with light. The real cause is friction,
But Simic's got this other system working.

And indeed we get somewhere, to Treasure
Island in interstices of leisure.

—7-23-95

I'm sitting here at Meineke's Discount Mufflers
While The Boys are dirtying up their collars
Fixing my car. Oh, how a poor guy suffers
He has to spit a hundred & 95 dollars!

For a goddamn muffler. I came a half
An hour early, by mistake. I have
To write a goddamn poem! The Golden Calf
Is causing me to have a cow (to calve).

Ah Calf! Hysterical, bawling little fellow!
'Twas thought you got aced out away back then,
When folks preferred Jehovah to your yellow
Material gleam, but—whoa there—think again. —

Just peel back the beard of old Jehovah,
Find some veal; he ain't no supernova.

—7-25-95

Local names poems for Mom at Jane's

The buffalo peas (or golden banner) bloom
Along the Golden Eagle Placer. Jane
Explains Last Dollar, where the valley's room
Tilts up to Timberline (a rocky gain).

Off west War Eagle, Golden Fleece, & Key-
Stone 1, 2, 3. The eastern lodes are Senate,
Ruby King & Banner. Rosebud. Whee!
I love each mountainous name; I love to pen it.

Downhill from Klondike Mountain, Rosebud Mine-
Dump. Then the road. & cabin. Columbines.
A couple clouds, pure whiteness clumped & fine.
Some remnant snow! under the lodgepole pines.

Strawberries, hummingbirds, Grandview, Rainbow Lakes!
Three-Jacks Placer—endless—Goodness Sakes!

—7-29-95

Poetry Reading Video

"Thank you—Good night." Thus Isla Cross begins.
Quiere decir, "Buenas noches"; we are off,
Amateur images, loving words, the pins
Drop with the "aura" of Verb Stroganoff.

Ilya Kutik (Anselm, Lyn), exotic
Russian ghost-debate*, then Ide Hintze,
Surrealistic crooner of the vatic
Impulse, like a European Quincy.

Then me. Then Rewind. Then the very last
Event—I play through Norma, Levi, Rosemarie
& - we hear Alice Notley with a cast
Of thousands (words) create a jamboree

Of tragedy filtered through intelligence,
Radical music made of perfect sense.

& vice versa.

—7-31-95

*See 7-6-95, on 7-1-95

Language is like a weasel shot with scars
diagonally, as if from far below, neon-seeming
afterimages revealing bluish-white to be
the formal speech of rolling landscape

—6-4-80

PART IV

The Red Triangle of Poetry

(elaborating on a quote from Judith Simmer-Brown) 17 April 2008

MESOSTICH

I was swingin' on a
s T ar
(it ' s not too
damnably ea S y, y'know) one day, when

some minor G od
l O ped past &, stutterstepping,
O ped the Pearly Gates
of his D entition to

con F ess
s O mething about the nature of
contemplative R eality. I

U nderstood him well, though
he S pake in

A
bizarre L ingo composed of Polish consonants,
grunts, and yode L s; some fluttering Black-Hole dialect.

T his was the
semantic gist of his O ration:

" B alance is
(almost) E verything. (pause)

A ND

a L ong the edge of
balance, there's a bunch of I mbalance, BUT
T he main
T hing most
people forget is to ba L ance their balance between
balanc E & imbalance! Etc.!" He turned a cartwheel
or two.

" O h," I said, "I see.
One F orgets to
follow that F lash of insight out to
the overlap of Galactic and General - Electric, the appliance
of perfect C are to the imperfect but
E xact
structure of Carelessness!" The god N odded. & grinned.
T hen -- woops -- he (or she) slipped on a
patch of antimatter and w E nt crashing through Space
around and around and all a R ound--and I think I
see him (or her) sailing
by still from time to time,
and I smile and
wave
(or particle).

ʎarch 19, 2006

SUNDAY CAMERA

BLONDIE

By Dean Young and Denis Lebrun

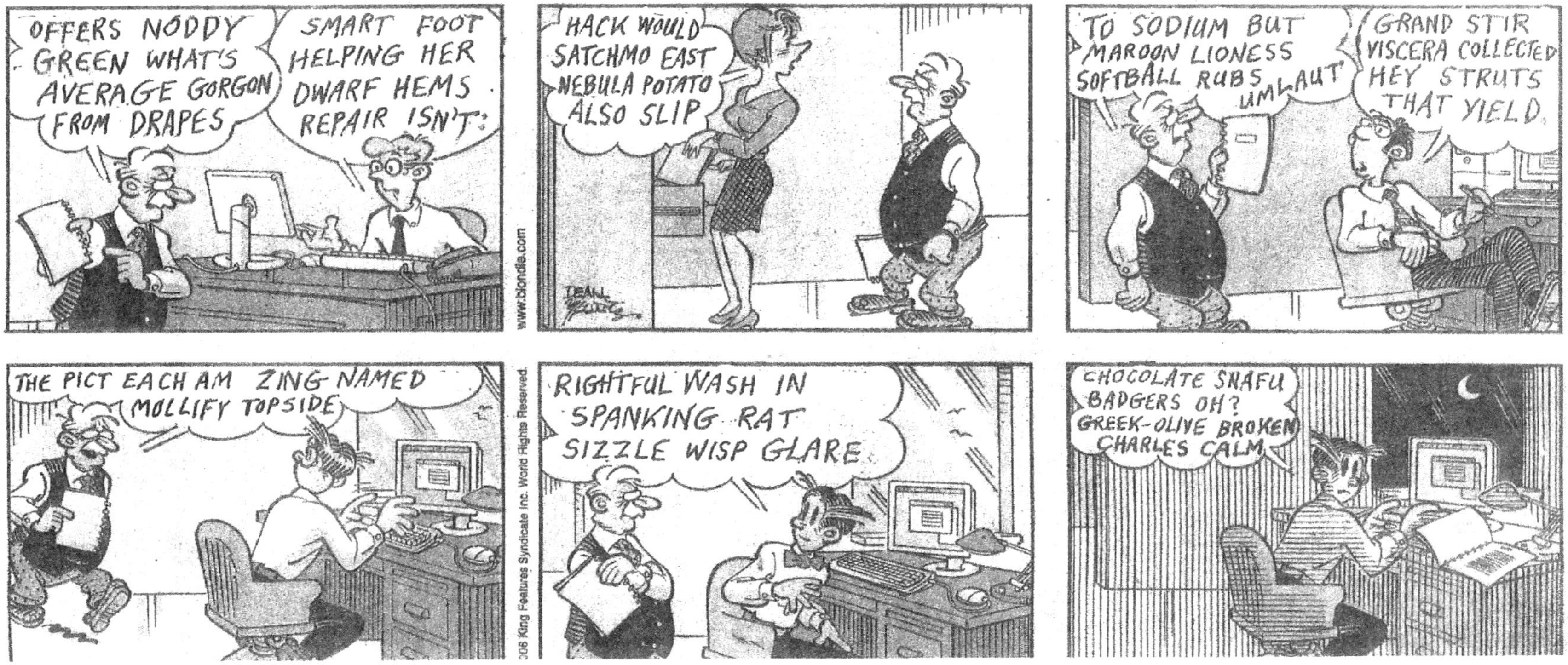

"MUD BARLOW"
Peak Water
Where has all the
actually
actually
pumping pump dump...... pull this water up
watercrunchers think of as an X

massive unglassy Cassiopeia's anarchy waterwater
Mexico is actually sinking into itself

face what we're dealing with
major source
conflict
Tibet
hotspot
Global Water Future
water water
wilderness
peasants around the world
fortress ownership confiscated
Nigeria distrump
Suez, et cet
Run their programs.........

"Orange Farm"
bottled water mass insanity pure fucking greed
fossil fuel intensive & tense intense yes

NUCLEAR POWER DESALINATION (poison brine)
"Corporate Water Cartel"
It is the FACE of Climate Change
Lake Titicaca ha!
trillion trillion trillion trillion
*syllable syllable syllable
voice like voice like voice like

water

if Mud would talk & talk & talk
on & on & on
u s w
the water of the world would be
refreshed reversed reborn revived
syllable syllable syllable

myth of abundance

V A R I E T Y

Aug. 2016

Very soon

After the

Rum,

I realized

Everything Everything

Tastes

Yummy.

L ifting
T I me
F rom
TIM E .

12 January 2014

A S ome
L ike
I t
C ombed
E rect

.   /
, ,   --
min   but
emit   time
times   emits
time's: almost
letssgo: -------
let's go   eternity
where to?   let's go!
also: when   perfection
to go is...   = beginning
cast a spell   and location
the occasions   is over there
and so forth** simultaneously
can anything happen only once?
events can be ordered, measured
the only absolutes are half-real
you write c & then you write lock
repetition and/or near-repetition+
before you can say Jack Robin a day
so what's an intellectual structure?
between any 2 events lie more events#
why cannot everything happen at once?? etc.
squeezing what we want into machines[0]
what's wrong with a circular definition?
plants started to live cyclically like000
if time can be unreal, how about: thought?
INABILITY OF THE MIND TO COMMAND ALL SPACEx

When all is said and done, no perfect accuracy exists.

A circle on the walls, based on sun, not on us.

THE END

the end

CUP

My black coffee cup. Black in the light, blacker in the shadow. My tablelamp's just above it, causing two thin arcs of light along the rim of the cup. Moving my head left and right makes them sneak around the edge, as if they were slowly dancing. And when I raise my head—as I just now did—I catch an exciting little double-arc—thicker, shorter—where the coffee, the cold, black coffee within the half-full cup, meets the inside, curved wall of the cup. Of the strong, the dark-the-more-I-look-at-it cup.

The cup is simple. Dark and stark. Plain ebony. Writings or pictures on it would be frivolous. It has a handle, a no-nonsense grip. "Grab me," the handle seems to mutter, "if you want to pick up me and my cup." Little gleams of light adorn the handle, but it doesn't care.

I've placed the cup on a white piece of paper. The cup just casts a shadow on the snowiness of the paper and stares into the distance. When I pick it up again, it is unruffled. But as I turn it in the light I can see a world of variation *on* and *in* the cup. Drips and scrapes and smears, besides the ever-hungry lamplight. Specks and reflections. Who knows what's inside the hard, sable substance of the crockery itself. Focus. But not a bit of color. Unless —

SOUND WALK 2:15—2:45 P.M. AROUND THE HALF BLOCK 3-24-2014

light footsteps on porch
oxygen puff (one entry)
purr / hum—passing car (won't note each)
cane on porch
doorslam (far away)
distant traffic (downtown)
paper rustle
chickadee titter
cane rubs on coat
slow shoes on stone path to sidewalk
house sparrow chirp
black car idles…
black car revs off
(variations of tires on Pine St.)
whacking a can (next block)
(I turn right)
chickadee-lite
white Via panel truck drives by (19th)
starling twitter, whistle
house finch spring song
(turn down alley)
incidental pebble-kicking
walk (left, right, etc.)
unidentified bird twitter
car brakes… and again (19th & Spruce)
hum,,, purr,,, twitter
twist of wind, left ear
chick-D *song*
my sniffle
pebble walk
(note—I notice more sights, too—irregular
pound scrape rattle small white fence)
caw caw caw
caw caw caw caw
whoosh (cat?)
man rummaging in pickup bed
caw caw caw caw caw
bicycle tire sound (18th St. surface)
chug (?)

[stepping out from
the house and
heading streetward]

scrape caw
distant rrmm
rev (ntense)
purr
paper flutter
wind chimes ! * %
thump (across street)
papers flutter
rev—
caw
Pine St. cars, again
sparrow, sparrow
flicker call
dogbark
unidentified click
more flickers
cane in dark green plant leaves
cane on porch
key scrunch

SUNNET

for Peter Warshall

So bioluminescence is rebellion;
I'll take more of that for danger's sake,
For danger CHANGES spots, a "leopard" hellion:
Local beauty's always on the make.

I mean, I mean, review iambic swing
From lip to line and back again—half dead
With poison from excessive light (the Sting);
But white reflects while black absorbs, and red

Is Long enough to govern half a life.
Enchanted by the sun, this bullseye range
Refines itself in terms of tonal strife,
Which livens up romance: home *in* the change.

Do shadows merely blot the multitask
Of shifting hues?
(You thought I'd never ask.)

COLORADO BLUES   3-24-2014

        S o, do these buddy-buddy disorders
D   E stroy us via
E   N capsulation, or maybe rot a-
M   I d the mentalities, or perhaps due to
E   L imination of feeding structures (better known as
N   I hil-blood-grub-ism)? Or, especially Out West here, from
T   T exas Tyler singing one too many "Remember Me, in the something of a
                Long long day"?
"I   Y ou?" we remonstrate vociferously,
"A   nd where's your motherfuckin' yodel, Cowboy?" as the mountains
                hiccup into nothingness.

Part II

        S plash that Midlothian sandy-beach
D   E ssert over my wayu, Herb; th-
E   N we kin suck up Lake
M   I chigan's sister-in-law till all H-
E   L l breaks luz, while Momma keeps on
kN   I tting "up" Chinese solutions to stu-
T   T erstep commercialization. Yes yes yes all the skin,
I   Y earn for that little brown spoon with a sky-blue speck in it which
                is pure shadowless
A   merica.

25 SOUPS 5-19-15

fat-as-a-hippopotamus-leg soup
walking right up to that wall soup
you are totallynutsoid soup
Tom water of the tomato L. grampus capital B soup
mesa-to-redleaf soup
"carp" jiggles soup
hey-let's-and soup
pickled rhino feet-juice—uh—soup
garments of the impoverished white soup
sliced-leg-muscle soup
glass of pure fresh water soup
King Zog of Albania's "favorite" soup
60-year-old Iowa-hickory soup
your grandmother says, "why-not?" soup
crack-a-dealio soup
the messed-up Peterson dog soup
large Smash artillery soup
which dish ledger into soup
until Kraft larch soup
Abie pick a block soup
paragon that bluestuff comma soup
beat you up Book soup
vagaboop poop soup
Page 3 soup
John Dillinger's one-ad owlark soup

FOR ANSELM HOLLO

(After seeing George Quasha's film) 30 January 2013

POETRY IS...

Art made of language (without added music). Thus it differs from other arts,
because its medium is a code, rather than basically physical substance
as is the case with music, dance, even painting and architecture, etc.
So, for poetry to be an art, a lot of extra mystification is necessary, to
bridge the gap between system and thing.
Backtrack: though language is larded with denotation and a grammar schema,
it is indeed an organic substance. It's the fringe of what we call
nature, the skin of ecology; it's squeak deliberation. It just grew.
The marriage of brain, heart, tongue and larynx. You can smell trouble in
that menage.
So poetry's language gratia language. Which like everything else in this
little squib is open to contradiction. I mean, it's made of meaning
as well as unmeaning. It's not so much in between (though it *is* that
lovely spacing) as both at once. All 3. All 4.
And, re "is": it includes is (poetry does—it's the thinnest universal
inclusion), but *it's* so to speak, every fucking transitive verb
instead of the to-be family.
It's play. It plays. We look and we see melody. We listen and we hear shape
and color, parallel variances down to subatomic size, which we divine
atheistically. Smell / the touch / of taste.
Since any poetic "move" begins hardening into an announcement of itself
within a few split seconds of its birth, poetry needs to rip itself to
shreds every moment. But of course that very "need" IS a veritable
illustration in a textbook, so we go for the opposite and the slant
opposite, and so forth. I mean, "etc." Echt.
Poetry is the Little Bang that heppns in a relatively homogeneous word-
universe. The celebration of slight differences and so forth. Planets
& all.
Poetry is the nervous system's nervous system.
The há-ha-ha in a laugh. The "if" in "life." The "f" in life. A. Not this,
this.

PART II

Poetry is not "poetry" but it can contain a few shovelfuls.
Oh hell, poetry (words) is an interesting graph of tensions between surprise
    and the expected.
Poetry is song unsung.
"Why do I look so ugly?" could be a line in a poem.
"Carrot s s s" could be a line in a poem.
"Th" could be a line in a poem.
It all depends.
You just gotta keep your many definitions of poetry moving in relation to
    each other.
But poetry's gotta sing. Luckily, the word "sing" bubbles in & out like
    billy-be-dust.

Poetry's a wet ocelot rolling in the grooves
between your samovar AND deep-sea
diving into atchoo! Bernadette's living-room.
Rollie rolie hrbicek went o'May.
wood minus.

poem

luns lungs lungs lungs lungs lungs lungs lungs lungs
lungslubngslunvgfslungslungslungslu
luingslunglunglungklungl
lungslungsl

10-23-15

lungs lungs lunslungs
lunas

lungslungslungslungs;ungs;liungslungslungvfslu

glumlu lu un

lunge lungslungslungslunsgslungslungslungs;kllungs ul ul

lung lungsl lugluglugl;igluglug.ug

luingslungs dungslungslungslungslungs loooong

lungsi LARGE lungslungslungs

legs longs lungslund luingslungs l

unununun -- lun lin letsl ungs

lungslungsu lungs ¢ @l

ookungs ungs ngs gss !!!!! intricate

lungslungslungslungs lungs lu

Lungs stretchlu

fingers

lungslungslungslungslungslungslungslungslungslungslungslungslungslungslungs lungs

die lungen die Lungen die Lungen die Lungen die Lungen die Lungen the lungs
fleshflash lalalalalalala Large LARGE looooooong lungslungs in

LUNGS HAIR
LUNGS
LUNGS
LUNGS
LUNGS
LUNGS
LUNGS

lungslungslungslungslungslungslungslungslungslungslungslungslungslungslungslungs
... the lungs lungs lungs lungs lungs lungs lungs lungs lungs

Luft air

C omposts
O rdinary
P eople: ta =
D A!

C louds
O f
P arisianesque
D emise

C ollom?
O h
P erhaps a half-
D ecade.

C ruising
O nly
P artway
"D owntown."

to C ompost a short acrostic out
O f an existing acronym
P resents aesthetic
D ifficulties.

C omplacency taking that looooong drag of
O neiric smoke, cocking an eye, eying the
P lace called Out—combustible old party
D ays. New sentence: Hello, Dali (lulu). Hfx.

C ome all ye young (old?) fellers that mainly follow the C, lazy;
O rganize selves to continue P & D, namely,
P ull my
D aisy.

Cigarettes On Parade, Dudes

C oming into my late teens, my brelliousness spread to include premature
"O rnaments" of "Adulthood" and didn't realize that yoking those two
P romotes
D ecaption.

C an I match my mother's lonegevity of 92? No. I'm
O nly a few annu-circles away from that semi-Methusalehic chrono-
P ile, but Phillip Morris
D one begun to bring me down.

C hronic
O bstructive
P ulmonary
D isease.

C ode
O r
P erchance
D emonstration.

C ome
O ut &
P lay,
D arling!

C orrect!
O n it!
P erfecto!
D ead.

C uts
O ut
P ersistance
D aylight.

C onstantly
O fficial,
P artly
D elirious.

C ough!
O rchestra
P articulars,
D uh.

C ostly
O rganic
P olice
D epartment.

C losing
O ff, just this
P iece of advice :
D eify lungs. l l l l l
u u u u u
u n u n u
u g u g u
u s u s u
u u u
u u u
u u u
u u u
u u u
u u u
u u u
u u u
u u u
u u u
u u u
u u u

TWO PRONOUNS & THEIR FRIENDSHIP 11-20-05

Wild
Egg Under
Scrutiny

West/
East Useful
Synthesis

Will
Endeavor Umbrella
Platter

Watching
Eagerly Ultraviolet
Speck

Wishes
Electrified Usurping
Self

Work's
End Utopian
Sink

Word of
Engagement Unique
Set

With
Each` Un-
Safe

Wistful
Enterprise Utter
Sense

Poem 15 July 2015

Gathered

Altogether,

Rubbish

Becomes

A

Golden

Enterprise.

loving
words
gently
captive
greetings
heart
bigger
then
terrified
petrified
appeared
your
the
soul
every
three
composed
have
heart
reply
burning

The Regular World
for Jenny
love, Jack

1-18-16

H ere I stand,
A bove the egg-shaped bowl,
P ointing my
P enis down into a
Y awning toilet.

M y left hand has meanwhile turned
O n the nearby faucet so that I can feel (via
M arvels of imagination) the rush of water nearby
E nclosing, so that my member will
N ot now fail to join
T his universal flow.   &
                    There it goes!

Six Fart Acrostics 4-8-85

From
Ass
Rises
This
Fizzers
And
Reverbera-ting
Toots
Fresh
Air
Recoils
Timidly
Friends
Arise
Remarking
Ta-ta
Falls
Apart
Rapidly
Though and
Finally
Animal
Rituals
Transcend

PART V

ECO-PO

a few sowings

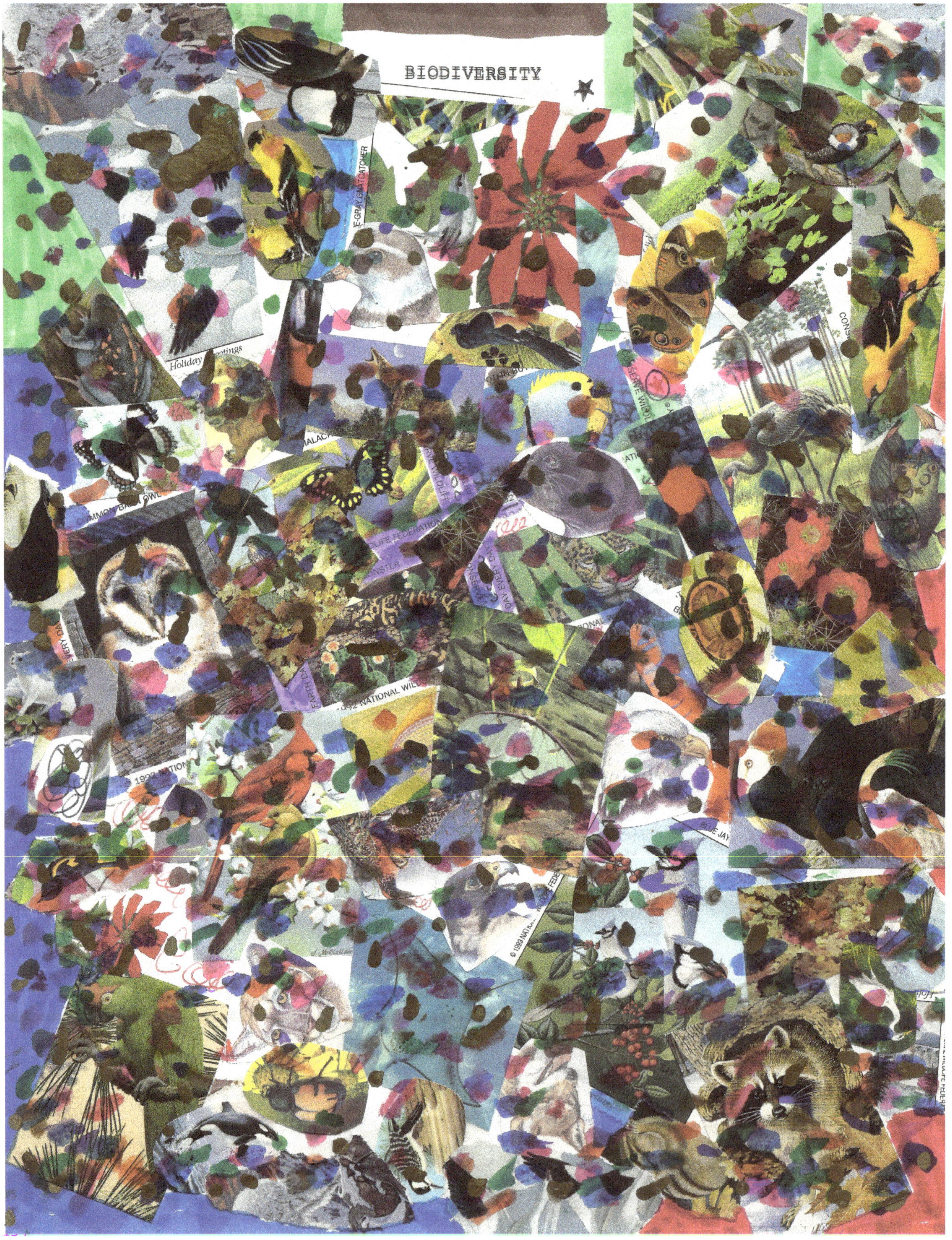
BIODIVERSITY

PROGRESS

Abracadabra!
Beauty rises up to
Collide with the
Devil! Or? Cooperate? Whatever. Anyway,
Earth gets
Flipped off by such
Geomantic
Hullaballoo.
In the various
Just sizes of that poignant,
Kinetic *onliness* called
Life,
Mothering powers
Nuzzle constantly into the
Open airs of
Possible gesture, however
Quixotic, towards the cosmic comfort of *eternal*
Reproduction
Sashaying, dancing, popping colors & multi-scale
Theories
Under the putative, relative, mandatory curved
Veneer of the
World, the
  eXcellent
  Yellow core we
  Zip arabesques about.

RECIPE ... FOR A PLANET

Take one batch assorted "people" gov't-issue.
Drop on island in Great Sea of Anywhere.
Snip mouths into faces, implant stomachs.
Paste on hands.
Stuff heads with goo. Label it / "brains."
Push chests up & down till breathing starts.
Set units on feet, turn em loose.
Drop fish into coastal waters.
Stick trees in ground.
Drop birds into atmospheric overlay.
Shake in animals, vegetation of all sorts.
Start wind machine, initiate rain system.
Sift total into homogeneous seething mass.
Watch people gobble/gobble/gobble.
Watch big brains invent machines.
Watch em use hands to make hands obsolete.
Watch desire spread like an ocean.
Watch rocks crumble to soil & get washed away.
Watch people invent clocks, & forget time.
Pepper with conceit.
Salt with greed....
Spice with impatience.
Simmer.
Raise temp. to 350° F.
Stir with cannons & skyscrapers....
Watch life dissolve.
Eat it up. You're the cook. You're God.
Move to another island.
Start again (cooking makes you hungry).

NATURE

Nuts
Air
Trees
Ungulates
Rhinos
Easter eggs

Nobody
Actually
Thinks
Ugliness
Really
Exists

Namby-pamby
Advocates
Trying to
Unravel
Republican
Essence

Nanook
Ate
The
Underbelly:
Repetitive
Ecstasy

Nap
Alp
Tip
Ulp
Rip
Elk

Newly
Arched
Thought
Undermines
Royal
Ennui

"Nothing"
At all's outside
This
Universe, yet it
Radiates
Essentials

Nietzsche
And
That other guy Schopenhauer
Urged
Radical
Elitism

Net
Aggregate
Truth
    Unties
    Regular
    Experience

Nuzzle
Arch
Trot
Unite
Ramify
Erase

Not
All
Time's
Under
Relativity
Eh?

Nerves
Actuate
This
Utterly
Rolling
Elegance

N o one's
A t home.
T he
U gly
R ealty is
E vanescence.

N o,
A ce,
T he
U rine
R ip
E lapsed.

N ewly
A rched
T hought
U ndermines
R oyal
E nnui.

N arrens-
chiff
A tlantis
T urbans
U rn
R homboid
E agleshit.

N ewspeak
A ctualize
T rend
U rgent
R elationship
E conomy

NATURE
ATUREN
TU   NA
UR   AT
RENATU
ENATUR

JUST TO SAY (AFTER WCW)

Hi there, Mother Nature, it's me!
Homo sapiens!

Just wanted to tell ya:
                    Sorry
        'bout all the
Destruction,
y'know,
billions of trees, butterflies, wild mice (at least animals
                don't have *feelings* for Chrissake),
water, air, soil … all that
stuff a yours.

But it was actually terrific—I mean
really fun to do.
Gimme some more!

DIRT 10-31-15

Dirt
Is
the Real
Thing.

Do
I
Readily
Turn into it?

Down
In the
Rocks, their eventual
Truth.

Did
It
Rain
Today? Look.

Don't
"Investigate";
Run your hands
Through it.

Destiny
Is
Relatively
Trite: growth, death.

Dirt
Interests
Roots?
Try tossing it away.

Destroy
It &
Regret your
Tackiness.

Delicious, nutritional,
Impressive, kind.
Royal and humble.
Tame & exotic.

Sonnet, 2016

Econo
mist
Ecolo
gist

Economists: they don't consider time
Beyond a handful years, because they don't
Expect to get attention 'less they rhyme
With "times" instead of time itself. They won't

Include ecology in reckonings—
Although ecology not only   is
Economy's ground—as much as things
Are ever ground of thought, ECOLOGY whiz-

Zes past Economy's edge (ontogeny's ledge),
Becomes apparent as the everything-word
In which econo-ME has not the heg-
—Emony of a bubble.   Poof.   Absurd

To think Big-Brain could ever've wrought (or bought)
Millennial meat; such thought be bound for naught.

Economists are unclever (wow)
You can't do Now
Without sniffs of forever.

& one more look:

economist	ecologist
Existence of	Equality ontological
Cash	Can
Opens	Open
Nothing &	Life,
Only	Or so
Money	Goes
Integrates	Its, her, his
Such a momentary	Story, every breath of
Truth.	Time.

27 February 2013

EVOLUTION

E ach birth's trajectory
V eers and ramifies all
O ver the possibilities of
L ove, etc.,
U ntil most of the identifiable surprises have not only popped,
T hey are
I nterior,
O nly to reappear as cheekbones shaped like a capital J, long leaf-locating
N ecks, random brown spots on the belly, or tendencies to flash the eyes
        open very quickly during sunrise.

(written in an 8th-grade class ((teacher: Val Wheeler)) at Casey Middle School on January 14, 2011)

RECIPE FOR A GREAT BLUE HERON

take
a long string of gristle
3 lbs of body
raincloud feathers
a couple handfuls pure claw
lemons with black spots for eyes
a long Damascus sword
2 huge heavenly-blue blankets
squawk like a railroad train
2 long willow sticks

pin the gristle on the little body
shape it to a graceful curve
sprinkle gray-blue feathers all over
stick the lemons in the top end of the gristle
jam sticks into the underside of the body
then glue the handfuls of pure claw on their bottoms
pin long blue feather on head (upper end of gristle)
sew huge blue blankets onto body
next, with *slow* electricity, get them flapping
activate squawk box
jam long sword into front of head, split it lengthwise
place appetite-for-fish-&-frogs medicine in sword-beak—tickle it to swallow
pour life-dust over the whole thing
watch as it flies off into the sunset
swallowing a delicious young crawdad

4-22-16
Earth Day

House finch song dances
across the back alley
into the
blue-white sky also
white blossoms
blow in from the left
house sparrows
*chirp

The geometric, many-sided, strongwood desires
of the trees
to radiate clearly up, but
touched with green…
I cock my head (ha)
to where Nan & Jen are talking
and I can't
see past
the apple tree
dressed as it is
in two thousand (2000)
glorious (yes, glorious)
B L O O M S

circle, no, circus [
Sun gets hotter
red metal chair stacked
over there
long silver ladder on the shed roof
rr train yodels / growls eastward
house finch again, systemic
one little white cloud
evaporates, like Oh

Part II

butterfly sketches a fast, low path
paving stones look like lavender in this light
two large / gray buckets on the little table
wasp

Earth Day Earth
Day Earth Day Earth Day
Earth Day Earth
a lune
alone
in the poem,
home

Earth day
today
worth
day mirth
day

Maybe
It
Ripples out of
The
Hands hearts and…

HUMAN EVOLUTION IN ACTION

3-25-13
1-24-15

throw rock
kill rabbit
build a fire
cook salad
make rabbitskin scarf
paint bison on rock wall
teach baby to hunt
put corn in the ground
remember it
slaughter the mouse-eating hawk
pave road
make a war
conquer diseases
marry the boss's daughter
bulldoze woods
excavate coal
mow the lawn
murder all insects
frack
lend money
advertise

6-9-01

REALITY AND NATURE

snow leopards

The basic thing (if not the basic act)
is the painting of the snow leopard
in the Biz X restroom.
Biz X, by the way, stands for Business Express, and
that painting is *very* realistic.
Also big, and under glass. When I,
being male, stand taking a leak
in the Biz X restroom toilet, I'm
almost immersed in the snow leopard
picture for a minute. At first I enjoyed
it; it's competently done; it shows a mother
snow leopard licking her cub's head.
One sees an undeniable love of detail.
The cub's head is *nearly* as big as the
mother's. The mother's tongue is
lapping out in just such fashion that
a shiny tooth is barely exposed. That
shininess is redoubled by the fact
that the picture's covered with
glass. The whole picture, in point of fact,
is a poster for the Denver Zoo. Well,
as I say, I enjoyed it at first, but
then, as I told Tallie, I really got
sick of it. The realism became very
bland to me, that kind of "bland" that
somehow has the energy to be incredibly
obnoxious. Tallie's this cute, skinny gal
who used to work at Biz X, though by
now she's quit and, I think, is living
in Denver with her boyfriend, though
they may have moved to LA or something. In any
case, she didn't even *know* the painting
at all because she always used the employee
restroom somewhere off behind the job
counter. But anyway I did get really sick
of it, and I told Angel then (but she wasn't

acquainted with the picture, either). By
the way, the reason I'm in Biz X often
enough to have this kind of ongoing res-
ponse is that I'm always using their xerox
machines. They're not really Xerox xerox; I'm
using the term xerox in its generic application.
I have these poems which I write and then
I have to xerox them because I want to
send them off somewhere and I need to keep
at least one copy. I'm in there about once or
twice a day. But what I'm getting to/at is
this: that lately the painting of the
snow leopards (there *are* two of them, after
all) has, for me, lost its obnoxious quality
and become—not exactly just normal again
but even attractive! I like it in a deeper
way, even, than I did when I first saw it
a few years ago. In fact, I really dig
it. Even that shiny tooth interests me. Snow
leopards look like you could stick your
finger right through them.

LUNE SERIES (3,5,3) September '04

What problems does
a bee with a little
party hat present?

In the beginning
something fat spread, under the
harsh, dark explosions.

The dead cat
didn't bother them. They were
reading Jane Austen.

I see a
tiny fishing-boat filled with treasure
—now it's gone.

My fingernails constitute
a deck of available crescents
suitable for interpretation.

The warm, brown
substance soon covered the floor;
that was that.

In cladistics, we
strip a phenomenon down until
it's completely unknown.

But what of
that whiff last Sunday? Couldn't
we go back?

White? Circle? Gray?
Captain Rainbow pointed his telescope
nearly straight up.

It really is
a photograph of a brick
driveway, ain't it?

SONG   for Ed Sanders & Mahalia Jackson

to the tune of "Amazing Grace"

Appointed soil / sole ground of life
Slow growth since coastal dawn
        So recently your stuff was rife
        And soon O nearly gone

—

Eight hundred kinds / of birds delight
The North American air
        But forests're felled in a money-fight
        There'll be no nesting there

—

The western bluebird / sang among
The February sage
        Its warbles sweet were roundly flung
        Howe'er the snow did rage

—

A little liquid / trickles down
The thinness of the Platte
        A million burghers swell the town
        And that's the end of that

—

The fox squirrel's tail / jerks light as air
Shows feathery orange core
        The brown face dressed in short, flat hair
        Provides the either/or

—

"Hey, Mother Nature / Father Time
Is running up the road!"
        "He'll never come," she said in rhyme
        "Chronology's such a load"

—

The Cape May Warbler / wormed its way
Along the elm twig dead
        No insects in that woody gray
        But still its cheek was red

Mixed Flock FLIGHT: V Formation

Bold Indigo Radiates Dawn.
Beat It, Rosy Dynamite.
Breeze Image Ruffles Death.
But It's Really a Dream.
Brings Iridescence Right Down.
Bathing In Royal Dust.
Bitsy Intelligence Runs Dynamometer.
Bread Is Real, Damnit.
Breast Inspection Reveals Dwarves.
Brain Illness Resists Daffodils.
Be Important: Resuscitate Deities.
Budge Ionosphere or Risk Drabness.
Buckaroo. Instress. Rumpled. Depart.
Brontosauri Invoking Railroad Days.
Breathing Instigates Raving Demons.
Basic Incapacity to Recognize Darkness.
Burl Ives? Really, my Dear.
Backstroking Into Ravioli Dharma.
Breathtaking Interests Reduce Dullness.
Bestiality Inside Rice Doughnuts?
Big Ivory Rodents... Drowning.
Beetles Ice Relay Dada.
Bride Inserts Ravishing Dagger.
BOOM! I Rise, Double.
Booze Itch Ramadan Darn.
Butterbread Ingrains Radio Dangle.
Braggadocio Incites Reactive Dangers.
By Increments, Reading Darwin.
Blushing, Irrepressible, Rhythmical Daughter.
Branching Ironwood Remains Deciduous.
Blatant Irony Ready to Decipher.
Barbarians Insist on Righteous Debauchery.
Balance Isn't Representative Deconstruction.
Brilliantly Inked, Roy DeForest.
Bachelors Invariably Remember Deodorant.
Bulbous Indentations Reposit Depression.
Bright Ignominy, Roasting Desert.
Bad Inch Roaring Detox.
Black Imbroglio Rectifies Dice.
Bugs: Item of Rustic Diet.
BETTER INCORPORATE RAW DIRT.
Being Incoherent, Raunchy, Drunk.
Blow Illimitable Radiant Dithyrambs!
Bagatelles Include Reified Documentation.
Both Implement/Reject Duality.
Beggars Inscribe Richguy's Description.
Belly Id Revival Dancer.
Bleeding Iodine Rectum Design.
Bereft Internal Revenue Dog.
Brisk Improvement Replaces Delirium.
Butterflies Image, Ravens Drift.
Blurted Info on Radish Damage.
Berouge Implies Rouge, Daddy.
Blind Ichthyosaur Rips Dactylics.
Bless. Inlay. Repeat. Decode.

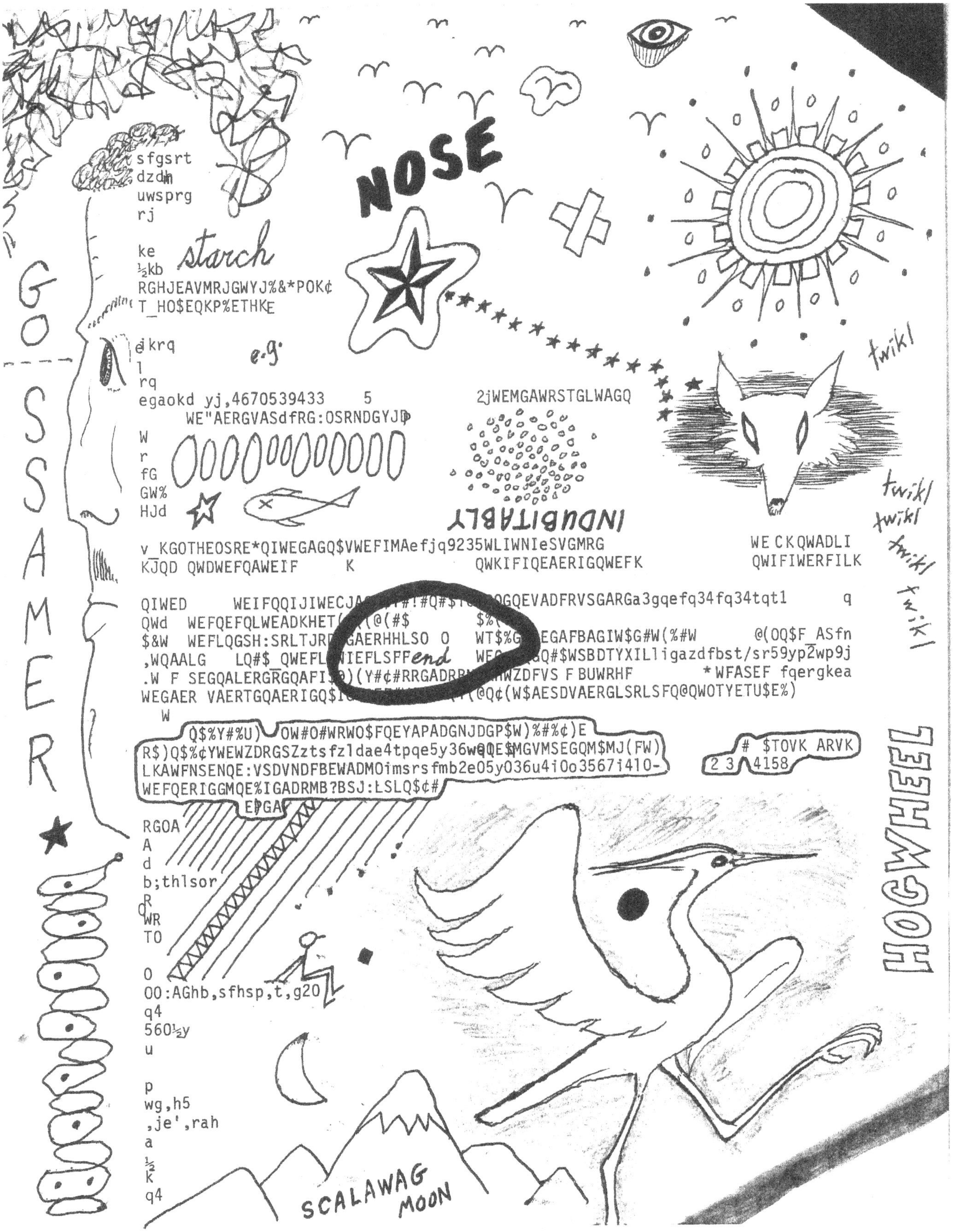

GOSSAMER
NOSE
starch
e.g.
INDUBITABLY
twikl
twikl
twikl
twikl
twikl
HOGWHEEL
SCALAWAG MOON
end
sfgsrt
dzdh
uwsprg
rj
ke
½kb
RGHJEAVMRJGWYJ%&*POK¢
T_HO$EQKP%ETHKE
ikrq
l
rq
egaokd yj,4670539433 5
WE"AERGVASdfRG:OSRNDGYJD
2jWEMGAWRSTGLWAGQ
W
r
fG
GW%
HJd
v_KGOTHEOSRE*QIWEGAGQ$VWEFIMAefjq9235WLIWNIeSVGMRG
KJQD QWDWEFQAWEIF K
QWKIFIQEAERIGQWEFK
WE CKQWADLI
QWIFIWERFILK
QIWED
QWd
$&W
,WQAALG
.W F SEGQALERGRGQAFI
WEGAER VAERTGQAERIGQ$I
W
WT$%G
*WFASEF fqergkea
Q$%Y#%U)
R$)Q$%¢YWEWZDRGSZztsfzldae4tpqe5y36w
LKAWFNSENQE:VSDVNDFBEWADMOimsrsfmb2e05y036u4i0o3567i410-
WEFQERIGGMQE%IGADRMB?BSJ:ŁSLQ$¢#
$TOVK ARVK
2 3 4158
RGOA
A
d
b;thlsor
R
WR
TO
O
OO:AGhb,sfhsp,t,g20
q4
560½y
u
p
wg,h5
,je',rah
a
½
k
q4

THE
POET
IS
IN

Part VI

DO A FEW

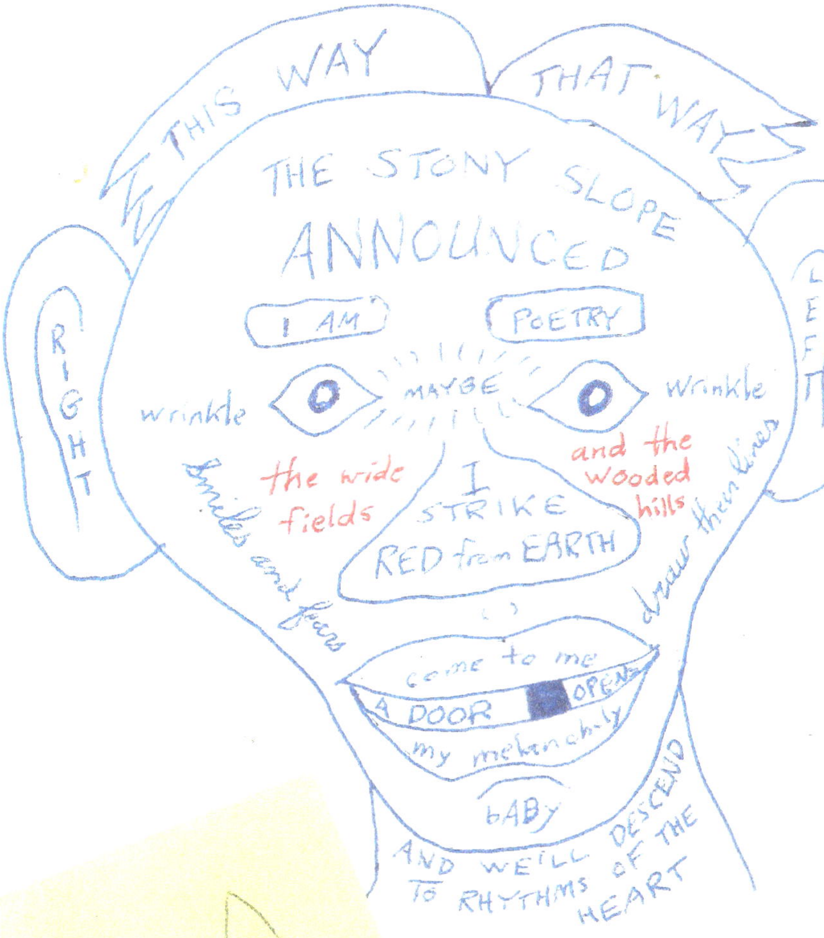

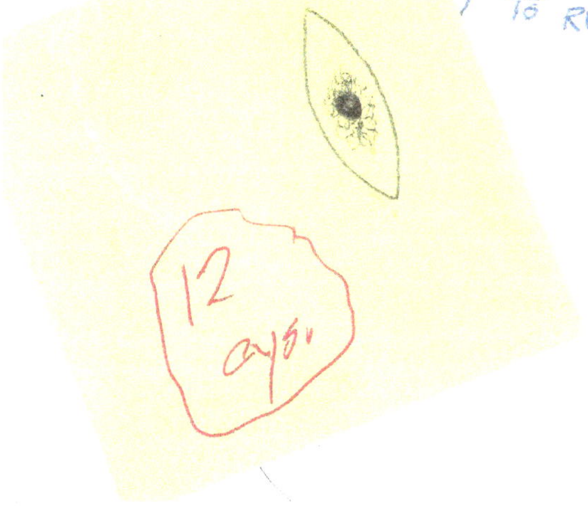

JAM 1966?

grell Barbiere die u dawgs sniffysnaffy cumbersome pickle 4 Hume
the bull tells talisman thomasman thumbes thumbells balls ove ste
merry R harry quidnunc erasure glacier a pleasure fall some ful
some sum Kwakiutl vespers or maelstrom with a lard whippet me buoy
up the scuppers of scuttlebutt no dying in the machines please Ur
cold idea old as chaldea dead mackerel sac of sarc k sargon of akkad
hewn nitehood wuz inflower borealis but don't be rude bot sail butt
batshit scut sail where there but everywhere allhere everywhichaplane
likely story whambam tkyou mm goobye she missed er chips furl what
thay mey down to the "c" in chips thoutit wegot Hips sail sail alll
donne back up A muskrat coma tomorrow whutz thet inn thuh rode a
head? but quail but sail butt billy that kum on boys quat billyclub
bud venue zail? under thiss is a? waking on the Nile walking on the
kingdom for a hippopotable liquine eos goddess ove hips & sailing
wax whacking on the we were spilling sails all th illness goober one
loose if ewe please sauntering lollygag whip ship dunbar chocolate
i wish butt the scales scootlebat quickass wink wink wink wink
i hear your cave mister earth short shrill shriek on leather works
where the snail wails inna swale ave a kind of gauge im guano go
back hoam a hwit cao moanz suitable bill sutter sequential cherry
key all them dry dust break it up sticks birds breed seven sounds
swound grand

down de road

22 April 2011
with Sierra Collom

a poem about growth

One pleasant forkful of jelly on *
my/life/is/all/I/can/handle/now//
Gummy reasons for everything, it
seemlikeexpansion'sactuallycrun
Chy-pond-fuzz-burps-on-fire.Go
deepcrunch&it d i v e r s i f
Eyes!!!Young goslings nuzzle
viruses@#$%especially%becuz
The preening lick is pasty
moreorless,andDNAsends us
its helix of maybes;home
dubldevildividing@each+
invisible width.Babies
w/subatomic:stinkeye[
Phlegm-dance-breathe
p$n$trat½thmystery(
glassfastenedmasts
=¼=microsquirrels
Taut-bellied boy
?zxcvbnmgrowths
Up+Up+Up+Up+Up
pleasant fork
chew&swallow
upthe swamp
full-green
oooooopen
wiiiiide
frmlism
portal
%%%%%
tone
yes
Uh
O

THE CITY SLICKER WITH DAN HANKIN

She thought …

Johnny Cash	was a pay toilet
Buck Owens was an	IOU
Roy Acuff was	some kind of allergy
Spade Cooley was a	castrated Chinaman
Kitty Wells was a	place to drown unwanted cats
Molly Bee was a	bunch of guys sitting around Granville Phillips lubricating screws
Hank Snow was a	judicial wig
Doc Watson was a	detective's helper
Leroy Van Dyke was a	truckful of the King's lesbians
Ray Price was	the cost of a sunlamp
Bob Wills was	how much somebody wanted to lurch about
Lester Flatt was a	pair of falsies
Ferlin Husky was a	big fella rolling up a flag
Red Foley was a	crimson horse
Little Jimmy Dickens was a	small prying tool that wouldn't work
Charley Pride was	white supremacy
Ernest Tubb was a	serious bath
Montana Slim was a	fat cure in the Rockies
Porter Wagoner was a	transportation company
Red Smiley was a	new lipstick
Faron Young was a	violation of the Mann Act
& Lefty Frizzell was a	new hairstyle for commies

BACK ON THE GRINDER AGAIN   APPROX. 1979

(writ in the regular interstices of a night's work on Hot Rolls, IBM)

tired legs & weightless heart & head
sure
intimacy the outmost frontier
ain't language's but
assassination's
nothing serious, just a white rose
as I realize I have to see
what flaws the hot rolls might have
buttered bread & butter dangled off a low hill
too much pressure in the thin atmosphere
for hands like skinned hermit thrushes
fit my shoulders to a sagging daytime
alone with a cup of moths
these stones are passive & stick in the railroad bed
but on some continual extreme
half-moon smile of the bow & arrow
we are animals with ten
percent uncomfortable ocean spray
but all aforethought
stuff in the state
a bighorn sheep in stream of attention
gray colors symbolize virginity
hopping from limb to limb of a groundsquall
easy to end there, like the ruptured duck
creates a soldier of a sort
I'm tired of my ego so I look at your legs
soft & savage as a steel surface
bleached in lawns of the moon
so that's a concession stand, a popcorn for you
& a treat I have to use as uniform
skid WW nearly done, no sunshine
evident upon the copier plant pines

side thoughts
crack up to be
but back to the clear clay gods of
insects, old ground, what do you know
in the sense of 'painted in a corner'

to ladders, of which there are none
sick wires grabbing you in place of dream
dignity is always out of place—when
you'll 'love it or you'll hate it'
after all is well & clear
after words killed with desire appear
conditions of scattered pinpoint rage
in the waters of management
I see that everything we do is ladylike
or not until nobody's fooled at all

I doubt everything
sinking through the land of
breakfast on the green jungle
lipsticked nipple messages of this
yellow sleep, lost among negative food
backing down from a human lettucehead
chickening out when the bone's met
slant of furies, helping me to two-step
the south is stuck in biped spirit like
red bugs on a marble statue
mountain railways in your glass of alum
as if the flesh were secretarial I see again your paralyzing lightness
flitting like a lizard in a house of bone
a goblet of stone equals happy question mark
so be serious, soothsayer
toxicity itself is innocent
I can't begin to tell you how I like your
love pops up in curves of space

XMAS

X
Marks
A (any)
Spot.

eXemplary
Merriment
At
Solstice.

X-ray
My
Altruistic
Soul.

eXtreme
Massage of
Aptitude for
Shopping.

eXuberant
Madness
(Anglo-
Saxon).

Xanadu
Manufactured
And
Sold.

Xenogeneic
Masquerades
Anticipating
Solarization.

eXalted
Marsupial,
Aka
Santa.

Xeroxed
Mummeries
And
So Forth.

eXcessively
Mesmerized
Acquisition
Syndrome.

eXstracting
Melody from
A lack of
Sun.

X-rated
Money
All about
Salvation.

eXtrapolated
Margins
Alter
Society.

eXtra
Makeup
Attacking My
Space.

eXistential
Mutability
Acting
Solid.

eX nihilo
Marathon of
Abject
Succotash.

eXpunging
Memory,
Accumulating
Stuff.

eXcremental
Manitou
Abandoned in
Sky.

X-factor
Making
Absurdity
Systematic.

Xanthippe
Marries
A richer
Socrates.

From LIME RICKEYS, tradeoff with Larry Fagin. A selection

There once was a woman from Spain
Whose features were shockingly plain.
For example, her chin
Sported hydraulic skin
And each eyeball resembled a brain.

A hummingbird mingled the sperm
With the smegma of my Uncle Herm.
Result: one fried egg
With a vestigial leg
And its hair in a Cro-Magnon perm.

Agamemnon could hardly believe
It when Dumbo flew out of his sleeve.
He faxed his friend Hannibal
An ununderstandable
Scrawl: "Pachyderms! My pet peeve!"

I love my eggs boiled in picante:
I feel I'm encircling Dante.
In the 9th circle fries
My legs and your eyes
Like a tableau of life in Ypsilanti.

O OUR CEILING REVEALING STRIPES   FOR LISA JARNOT

dark   light
O   warm brown living-room dresser! Loom
dark

O   black ashtray!
O   my wife's blue tennis shoes!

O   salmon-colored pillow

on the yellow couch!   O tin table!

O   my blood-red T-shirt
dark

O   insect song   white pen
light   dark   dark light
O   stained finger
light
O   dark finger feeling weight
light   light

Why I Was Late For Work 10-20-80

"just drivin' through the suburbs, sippin' beer, Boss

dreamin' about you."

HOLIDAY SONNETS   2000 A.D.

"meet me, in St. Louis"

My briefcase contains love
with a chance to make birdie :
momentito
oldsmobile girl

disease metaphors were among his? most
diamond-studded wonderland of more
getting half the performance fleece
vertical dolores, great bones

Fe in the eye of the perfect
of nature Ever known, substituting
over the case as well net
savings bunch of entonces,

tomorrow brother's murder
por el mundo caliente, talvez

(untitled)

look, nobody knows about this
(poor Frankie, deaf as a doorknob)
which just *seems* to multiply
both points and miles for the Wolf

coming up: top stories to
fail, which is to say, to separate
I'm a little teapot, this is my
flashback super jumbo jet getting high

eensy-weensy spider went up the waterspout
feel better with Move-Free, two bucks
completely on Mother Nature
with 95% coverage

warm up with ten squats
ideas like profitability, oil-based

PART VII

Seashell Hair from Mars 1980, NYC

with Sierra Collom, age 6
(word/word tradeoff)

"Hi, Hatfoot Church, how are your cats of life today?" Then even a mud person could do what nobody ever done, especially when everybody goes la-la down baked fence ripped material. Illness came sliding down a piece of fur and got chubby. Suddenly the water turned purple and sunk. Each dog mumbled grumbled because nothing worked there anymore up. This shock slowly turned into a woodchuck that sold a gargoyle that had two homes in Brazil broccoli to Flowers Lipton, licker of joker pops can-opener. Sierra and Jack and their typewriter Juanita Chocolate-milk took piano drops, Margaret's old chair and Harry's chicken hawk along down a family mudbank that hummed a silky worm. They went bugboo beddy-bye in Nowhere, Alabama, and shot one loudmouth wall. "Mama!" cried the old-man wall. For ten hundred reasons milligrams became people watchers in shallow water shops. Like your hot-dog parked on gravel when nobody hears nobody. So well did people think of lace carpool dawns, night seemed spooky as ghost ketchup blue with alarms. But where these rocks came, butterscotch turned the corner handy as a grasshopper. Well, not now. Pyramids India flavored grape search woods and gone breezes down dresses. What fun! The heat was trying cold above water manners wave-broken as dog dreams. Tack a tack a tack. Drinking wow caught bow-wow in crack. Shepherds movie drip-dripped up the drain making god-knows-what sick. Well done, chick, you are available now for doing exactly nothing but not stopping number nine what huh well like chair hobbies. You spit off, hardball. Socks hurt when they go to the wrong store. Goldfinches are lilting upwards as the washerwomen get older in their house of graveyard boats.

Why should Evolution be the one jaunty thing in the Universe?
Who's that coyote flying just over the Milky Way? It's you!
I like to walk behind you watching your straight legs move.
(The rest of the world's pretty damn low on entertainment)
I'd live on your moon, if the commute were a little less.
You were born where the water drains counterclockwise @.
Yr voice smoky choo-choo blues distilled to a warm day=
River of novel, wherein the water licks every granule.
Your genes are growing out of your head like antlers.
The bottoms of your feet are black with garden dirt.
I remember on the day we first met/I broke a glass.
Your garden's like a home-story by Salman Rushdie.
Living imperfection is the jubilation of motions.
Small brown eyes're nuclei of Earth the element.
You marched and sang and were tossed into jail.
Your voice is like a pecan pie at one sitting.
You've skipped through streets of La Paz./ ./.
(Sometimes one curls up in small white box.)
Way deep inside you a bone fire is burning.
Leading edge is covered with red feathers.
Spunk comes from tinder: to show spirit.
Whirling bravery around a blue teardrop.
"Yo digo que es Spanich," como la niña.
You're a stump-of-fire and a diplomat.
1 speck of blackness - & I can't see!
.You embrace the earthquake of logic
You're like blood, or the letter e.
We've jammed up a storm sometimes!
You're generous (of noble birth).
Bist du nicht my symbiotic loop?
A butterfly rests on your back.
JennyKate will you be my mate?
Wanna flop in a hole with me?
The sun behind one palmleaf.
Ha ha ha ha ha ha ha ha ha!
Vision of blue monkeyfuck.
Yo quiero bailar contigo,
Hands that enchant seed.
You chaw up applecores.
Typical one-of-a-kind!
Nobody's watching us!
I love your company.
Circles of dignity.
Mind, hair of fox.
Perpetual notion.
Plurality is it.
"Not my fault!"
Giver of brio.
Unquenchable.
Silverbrain.
I love you.
Soft lips.
A desire.
Up/down.
Family.
Lovey.
Like.
Low.
Hi!
O.
,

FOR JENNY

from Jack

1998

*
**
***
****
*****
******
****
****
****

2-2-1's 9-late-16

bite of cookie
on the left, but

"pitchers of waste"
answer me please

crummy? Not so

opening *his* vanilla
pamphlet merely repeated

that trill of Morton's
noticing dry tracks

almost (not quite) complete

once upon a
brown-looking house

Baby Louie was
not there yet

French, English, etc.

it made them cry
as if northern Minnesota

"Well, we ate the pickles"
Sam will fish up some more

(down on his luck)

after *some* consideration
she nominated "wheels"

it wasn't that
like painting the hospital

with a little one

the police sometimes
all minor factors will be

it's cream outside
half as slow

Spring 1980

bad timing

there's something real good about bad timing.
A square-jawed eskimo slowly turns his head
away, into the blue glare, eyes squinting
with anger. there's something beautiful
about bad timing. the mighty hero became a hawk
and sailed away north to find the three old women.
there's something about bad timing that
puts triangles of brown into your veins.
will the English sparrow's head ever be predictable?
yes, bad timing is the skipped heartbeat
of hundreds of rural napoleons.
last week our year's supply of
marble-colored snowballs just melted away.

bad timing II

there's something miraculous about bad
timing. one wants to be right half
the time, the other wrong. there's
something about bad timing true
and pure as busted rock. one be-
comes dense but the counterpart falls apart.
there's this about bad timing:
it sits. they maintain, they fight,
like a machine. bad timing is the lack
of blur in a man's face. They embrace.

bad timing FINIS

when the word splits on the nose
and the face is a husk because
the blood has moved away,
bad timing has been riding once more.

like milk pouring in a dirtheap,
or an italian portrait, or a si
-lent animal, you never know what bad timing
is going to turn to next.

bad timing, bad timing, you have robbed
me out of my silver. you have turned the sky
into a jerky hockey field
where nothing is warm but mind.

BULLSHIT

Just one of those hypnagogic divining rods. Number 1: what *is* bullshit?

Bullshit, O *shit*! No shit? Yes, it seems to be mush, culled and curdled, whoosh, from the bull. Shit. It's dull. No, not bullshit, but to be: ocean-ful of shit, I don't know. Dreams of shore, dash it all. But bigosh, bullshit wishes it were cash for hash. This slush...delicious sour mash.

"Bull," definition 6 (1640): "a grotesque blunder in language." And "shit" (fraudulent element?).

Strong, dark bullshit. Just laying there. Rough-textured, roughly spiral, like a devil-trap. This compost, food infused with body-work-juices. Fertility personified. In the grass, nightsoil, about to brighten the dry dirt with its melt. Substance, yes, but soft, puddle of goodness, mothering vegetation and feeling the future. Already, per se, full of life: look at 'em scattering over and through it. The little ones. Bullshit. With rich brown odor a fellow could live on. Look! Bay, chestnut, roan, sorrel, brick, cinnamon, ginger, hazel, maroon. Chocolate, cocoa, puce, mahogany. Walnut, henna, brunette. Tawny, terra-cotta, mustelline, dusky, auburn, fuscous, umber, tan. Copper, bronze, black and white. Friendly and fruitful. Yo creo que si, por supuesto, mierda del toro es un animal muy importante. An olio of down-to-earth reanimation. Fun to produce. Bullshit is continuity's diamond.

Incoming love tasted like respect when I was a kid, but looked like sound effects. Outgoing love tasted like fox saliva. I thought truth was *so* reassuring, like a distilled waterfall. "That's very nice, dear."

Maybe I did recognize that a life lubricated unduly homogenizes the light. Maybe we were both wrong (me and the rest of the world).

The main assertion of this essay is that bullshit is a necessary mystery-glitch in our lives, like our bodies are (even though it comes from our souls.). Truth wouldn't be the truth without it. In other words, truth is never "pure." Picture anything. Picture a potato. It's not just that bullshit is the dirt on the potato (ah, romance!). It's that the absolute truth of the potato "itself" includes stuff that is ineluctably uncertain. Whether this variability be based in the imperfections of perception and thought or whether it exists "objectively" is itself a little hootchy-cootch shimmy that cannot be stilled.

Shimmy shimmy. It didn't prevent me from feeling I could individuate like a nightingale in a black hole.

Any language is constructed (i.e., just grows) to forcevomit simplified thought. Poetry respects language as a fierce animal or a pack of animals with, in effect, its own five senses and 6 desires. But the minute Poetry formulates *that* it becomes hard and sere and its exactitudes are no longer *the* exactitudes. Partly this is because we don't respect time, and by time I mean, here, the distinctions between immediacy and a split-second afterwards, etc.

I recommend that everybody write poetry (and almost everyone can pen some magic talk, play with the blocks), partly to become accustomed to the happy marriage of truth and bullshit. Study language as if you're going to throw it a bone.

Bullets:

- Bullshit's in the hardest mathematics, waving little gossip-flags.
- Bullshit's got vitamins.
- Et tu, Bullshit?
- Bullshit's your friend (as friends go).
- Bullshit can occasionally transcend Earth's atmosphere.
- In fact, Bullshit backs a chemical in every muscle.
- Bullshit's just what it's cracked up to be.
- Bullshit's in the eye of the beholder.
- Bullshit's blinding when you lean your head to the right.
- Bullshit just adores time.
- Bullshit, O Bullshit, thou art like the Summer to me.
- Bullshit's closer to the truth than a *lot* of stuff.
- Bullshit keeps slithering, sliding, slow-exploding, nebulizing, amid the word "transitive."

Bringing
 Up
  Life
   Love
    So
     Hard
      It
       Takes

- Some's good, more's better.

BY WAY OF CONFESSION 3 October 2009

Once when Sierra was a baby I was out with her, carrying her in a sling and doing some errands, one of which was to deliver my former wife Traudl (not Sierra's mother) her child-support check. For some reason I forget, it was to be hand-delivered.

I came up on Traudl's house through the field behind, not far from the Mental Health Center, and, as I neared the house, I suddenly felt reluctant to confront Traudl with my new baby, even as I gave her funds to support the little boys.

On impulse, I laid Sierra down under a bush, went in the house, gave the check and returned. She was okay, sleeping in the shade.

ABOLISH
ALL BUT
BALANCE

•

UNDERSTANDABLE

Uppermost in almost anybody's mind these days
(Not to impute Platonic shape to space)
Desire (as if it were a thing) will blaze
Entre nous anew, prognosticating lace.
Replace it. Better yet, reply. Take pen,
then Slice its feather lengthwise. Do not wince;
The barbules are OK. They won't want then
And now conflated (nor will we). But still Prince
Northernmost can't fly, due to the ice.
"Destroy! Destroy!" He crackles an open-ended cry
As crisp as cusp of "noumenon" and "nice"
Because he's fairly reached convergence, on the fly.
Now Look! The days of space do blaze like lace
Embracing many circles, in any case.

6 January 2008

Have you ever thought, when the
qualities of formalism are up
for grabs, that formalism has its
richest possibilities where they
are not immediately apparent at
all?

Generally, the examination
of any face (voice) whose owner is part of
the inquiry will discover the
beating of doors creating dance
tables in its textures.

S hifting
W ave
A ppearance =
M icro-macro
P aradox;

F eedback
(O xymoronic)
R iver/tree
M utational
"A nything"
L ove:
I mperfect,
S urreal,
M arvelous.

GARDEN VERMOUTH … ON HEARING SOME CHICKADEE TRICKS 9-25-15

S INGING along, September birds spring a mess
O F autumn, with its turning, falling air
N OTHING can intercept for long unless
the N ERVES create their own incessance, bear…
"E NTERTAIN"ment meant to double truth:
T RUTH is, the brevity beautifies its youth.

A Story About Poetry 3-25-14

Once upon a time I was in Brooklyn, poet-in-the-schools, and showed the acrostic form to a first-grade class, prior to asking them to pick word or words and acrosticize them. A six-year-old girl named Stacey wrote the following:

B lue is a color, a
L ovely color that is
U nder the sun
E verywhere, even in thunder.

I show it to classes now, all ages (including elders), usually writing it on the board in red or green. I read it aloud, step by step, pointing out the mid-phrase linebreaks, then read it out loud again, slowly and with pauses. I ask them if it's a rhyming poem. They say "no," and I agree but ask them to find some internal rhyme. Sometimes they can't. I show "under" and "thunder," also "un" and "sun," "color" and "color" and "is" and "is," the neighboring v's (a poem this small forms a neighborhood). "There's a lot of rhyminess within this poem. It's musical."

I mention the blue / thunder kinesthesia, the line-to-line flow and tell them I think it's one of the thousand most beautiful poems ever written in English.

I read any class a number of various acrostics to open up their senses of what the device can lead to.

Once a teacher, after an acrostics session with some eighth-graders, while praising the session and Stacey's poem, remarked that it's not good poetry to begin with a statement of the subject's category ("Blue is a color"). I agree as a general thing that such a practice is too generalized and generalizing, but in Stacey's poem it "works." It's simple and brief, it flows without a hitch into the music of the rest. I think it gives us (hearers) a sound that is both elaborated and contradicted in the rest of the piece, like Charlie Chaplin bowing to introduce himself, or the apple growing on the tip of a branch.

BLUE was written just over thirty years ago; as with many other extraordinary pieces, I've not been able to contact the author since Stacey composed it.

Poetry for Reed Bye August 2016

vil spreadlap

P oetry us sand Wilbyboriole MAKEPEACE
O nly or orange willet "comma" grosbeak
fEear one-chipping sparrowing two Slash wu
T o broadwing updown dreque bath
R enaiss ance crossbillapproach one pipit
and Y ore you water skunk lesser gold flinch
Please fly Ah! but coopers; ° great gray yowl
See? ey see 5300
AAAAAAAACK

BILL WAS RIGHT

No ideas but in things.   NO
Ideas but in things. No   IDEAS
But in things. No ideas   BUT
In things. No ideas but   IN

Things. No ideas but in   THINGS.
No ideas but in things.   NO
Ideas but in things. No   IDEAS
But in things. No ideas   BUT

In things. No ideas but   IN
Things. No ideas but in   THINGS.
No ideas but in things.   NO
Ideas but in things. No   IDEAS

But in things. No ideas   BUT
In things. No ideas but   IN

TITLE: OKAY, WHAT NOW — LATE JUNE 2015

love song?

S tack
O f
acrostic — N early
N ew
E dges,
T ouching.

Why not a sonnet? Rhythm sprung, of course.
"To Spring." "To Fall." To falter, what the hell.
But-what's the wiggle's subject? Trojan horse?
That motion crammed with politics: (Liberty Bell.)

Naw, Sonnet *schon*, but let's-take-a-moment to find
A hairy emphasis. Pneumonia? Done.
A lover? Breakwater pie? Slow wisdom lined
With tiger teeth? … Ah, got it now. A nun

Such—no, a NUN. Continuance Given to God.
….. C'mon,/ I don't/ Believe/ in God (although
I WORship continuance)—
For "God" sub "nod";
For eternity***, twirl to lavish the Life of O.

NOTE: The above 4-liner (5?)
is to be classed as a close bud
of the octet.

INSERT: The method
involved here (inclusion of shaggy additions
in or
attached to a famously
down) may be regarded exact-quantity
as an xxx extension of the Miltonic long
syllable (e.g., "stren-
gth"), or as a hybridizing element (see
such crossbreeds as
wolf-dachshund, which instantly extend the hunting range
below the surface of the earth).

(back to the sonnet)

That's it. Sestet will rummage in the cellar.
Note: male burst, female maintain. They're like
A thunderstorm together. Well well / weller.
Tree. Cloud. 13-lined spermophile. Hike

couplet: Ahh—doda—Wlâ dy—UO/Bk: (luleh]-Sched—
lit lemur low wall l lipping lyrical release,

TOY
MIX
WHY

There once lived a nimble young nun
Who promised to find all her fun
In support of the Spirit
Without getting near it;
Or so she proposed to the Sun.

the nonstop process bet. perfection
& life (difference), which bounce bounce bounce
bounce… not that there's anything
to bounce on. Also, pause,
sandwich.

the life of O is, of course, slow circle/perfect/death…
the dot is O crushed the rest is breath

the circle says "goodbye,"
pronounced "O."

The Life of O

Coming at O in the alphabet's snappy
run, it seems like an emptiness, or
an offwhiteness. But somehow
not like a lack:
there's special dignity (from being nearly Death's
        perfection?)   The sound
goes on as long as voice (or echo can go.
The sight is perfect as long as the eyes
can still approach it.   Then,
I think, each thinker will find
a microscopic view of the surface (if it *has*
a surface), revealing a texture like that of the smallest
subatomic particle—revealing
universe and universes fanning back from each crack or dot. The
roundness of O seems ironic. Not that, in fact,
it couldn't be slightly oval. It could. It
seems to carry the idea of death (repetition)
and the idea of life (repetition). To caricature
O, I'd make it (dress it up)
into a fancy old lady, both kind and
arrogant (in the thin air where the two qualities unite).
I was invited to microtalk with two patches of ground
from the plane O is imaged upon,
one from inside the circle, the other from just beside/
it. (There were also many patches nearby
from both below and above the O circle but they seemed
to be so uncertain of their space that they were Too certain of their *place*.
            Contrary
to my expectations, the inner patch's talk
was actually macro, based on countless iterations and
little else, while the outer patch seemed to unduly
fade (yet concurrently reverberate) and shrink into the distance.
Eventually they both did headstands in the skin of a dot
which caused me to nosebleed and squat on
the neighboring N, where I faced so many directions at once
I couldn't help but dance,
though I wound up bloodless.
(Well, not quite.)
Dizzy, I glanced up. I saw a shifting lump of O's, and what I heard was "OOO."

scattered words

accomplished
beers
cardboard
denoting
egglike
fleshiness
“germanic”
horse-shaped
inferior
jewelry-3
kiss
Lester Flatt   milky

The Real Couplet:

goes

Is this a Trojan Horse? Open it up.
You’ll note Nepenthe holding a wooden cup.

JENNIFER late March 2013

J is for * juice * jenny * jangle * jailed * jamboree *** jardin *
jabberwock * jellyroll * jumping jewel * jocose * jumble *
justice * joy * juxtapose-jack * judgement * journey */* jay

E && excellent, & ecru & earthy & egretlover & elegant & edgy & eeyow &and
explosion, electric & exertion & edible & educating & either & elf yes
elixir & *embosom* & emergency* & empress & exotic, & emotive & enchanting as well

N (()) (naked) (Narrative) (native) ("Natural") (nectar!) (necklace)
() need ()neighboring ()neurons ()nimble ()nimbus) ()NOBLE ()nonbeliever
)nomad( )NOTE( )nun( )nutbrown( )nutritional( )nest( )nymph(

N % never % naughty % no % near % neatness % nag ^ Necessary % necromancy % neigh
percent nervewrack % NEW % next: now % nightfall % "noise" % Nonconformist % noodle %
nonstop % nonesuch % nosegay % "nothing" % novel % n u m b e r % percentage 98

I? idea? ice-cold? iconoclast? Insecticide? IDEAL? Ignition? it's illegal?
Illogical? ILLUMINE? imbroglio?—Immense? imperishable? impossible? INcense. important? Impudent?
/ incarnate? Inconvenient? Intrepid? irregular ?
indulgent? inedible? infectious?—INFINITE? inkwell? inside…?
inspired? / irksome? Intangible? Iridescent? intelligent. If

F @ fable@ fabric at flower @ factor@-from@-fairyland@ —falter—@ ferment@ FORM@
fantastic@ farm¼@ folly@ free@ face@ "failure"@ fright@ fast@ fatal?@ fault!@
fresh@ favor@ fawn-feast@ feathery()@ fence@ ferocious@ festival@ fury@ FUN@
fuse fringe fever fieldfirefightingfuckfindflameflash@
flicker@ flip, float@ future…@ fundamental@ more

E = encore = energy = enigma = enkindle = envoy [epic = equal = Eros =
erratic = erudite = escaped = esprit = ethical = eternal = etiquette =
eruption = Eve = environmental = enviable example = enlightenment =

R is for KATE reach K reconstruct A rose T *real* E riddle K rebuke A river T rabbit E
radiate K rain rain A radical T react E race K rigor A rebound T rainbow E
refuge K romance A ring T royal E rapid K rage A railroad T Red E
repentant K reporter A rejoice T raven E reform K runner-r-r A reveal T
resolve E rapture KATE

love, Jack

C O M P U T E R 9-18-11

a few anagrams (with brief analytical comments)

Mute crop
That the products of the computer are at last voiceless.

Cute romp
That, in some ways, however, their mechanical playfulness is a charm.

Temp cour
That the computer represents an abbreviated form of condensed heart.

Tromp cue
That it's really a signal for nature or anti-nature to trample upon our lives.

Ump Co. etr'
That the computer tends to implicitly judge (favorable) the existence of Capitalism.

Term coup
But that it snips any actual span of life.

Tromp eco
That it runs roughshod over the ecological understanding and cause.

Met ur-cop
That, in the computer, the most ancient, forcible regulator is encountered.

Re: mot cup
That what it's about is the establishment of parameters around language.

To pure M.C.
That the computer is the ultimate "introducer" (lacking substance of its own).

CEO rump T
That the Capitalist's rear end is precisely the place to plant a kick.

"Come, U R tp"
That it's a contemptuous invitation to be and remain toilet paper.

O pert cum
That it seeks to make us feel sexy despite our absurdity.

MP cut ore / roe

That a sort of epistemological military police has sliced away the "gold" of existence, or alternatively, life's ability to reproduce.

Cuter mop

That the computer is just a superficially attractive eradication device.

Tor emu PC

That even an ostrich climbing Mt. Everest is not politically correct.

ROTC me up!

That computers "elevate" us via a regimentation-type ethical thrust.

PM cot rue

That, afternoons, the computer-user regrets the lack of rest that the ever-busy machine presents.

"Um" to CPR E

That one properly hesitates to rescue such an "excellence" as this artifact manifests.

Comet pur

That it's a dangerous space-giant about to crash Earth, but masking this with a soft, reassuring sound.

PO REM CUT

That it's a post office of rapid eye movements slicing up our communications.

Comte Urp

That computers actually amount to an exotic nobleman who wants to gobble us up.

Opt M cure(s)

That people choose a thousand things at once.

Pet MO cur

That this domestication has the modus operandi of a surly dog.

Cro-mupet

That the computer is a crude construct seeking to replicate ancient human skills.

M puce rot

That the metropolis of computers is the color and consistency of an engorged flea.

"Om" PU cert

That the computer's mantra of ultimate truth is definitely shit.

Route MCP

That the road suggested by this way of life is a Manifestaton of Counter-Paradise.

Rote pep rots cum-cum

(anagram of COMPUTER COMPUTERS)

That, finally, programmed energy mortifies the life force.

(There are more.)

[The author, a poet and teacher, is (still) computer-illiterate.]

POETRY is: (collaged)

Following is a collage made from characterizations of poetry by schoolchildren.

Poetry is...
a slow flash of light
having a snake
in your room
and you don't know what to do
your mouth playing a trick on you
I look very fierce
when I finish I feel
temperamental
a bumpy world
a rainstorm just standing there
like your hand is coming apart
maybe poetry is poor
Ahhh, poetry, get out or else!
goodbye everybody
poetry has killed me ... poetry is
walking on the moon with the flow of going
backward and the motion of going forward
Poetry is like dirt rushing in your face
a monkey saying, O take me away!
a zoo of heads
a floor in the moon
books in a pool
cherries in the ears
Poetry is like the alphabet all talking at once
shooting a lot of ink
under a rainstorm
letting your nose run without caring
you get so mad you fly to the moon
electricity blowing through a telephone
bending lines

The curly mirror
Dot line Dot line Dot
zig zag Star
And on the hundred and first day it eats 101 flowers
Poetry is like whatever's falling on you
I'll just go along the road with my brain in my hand
1 chinup 2 chinups
3 chinups of poems
in a splash in a
crash I love
white snow that nobody can see but me
"Hello, Poem, do you want to make some raisin bread?"

"Let's make it."
Poetry … ticks as if it had a face
But what a funny clock that eats sandwiches with pepper and "he ha, he ha,"
but its eyes look like gloomy basketballs.
Poetry is a brain of love.
And finding a wall that can't be broken
We'll eat by candlelight!
And we'll dance like crazy.
Come and shake your body, come with me.
Poetry is nothing and everything all in one
People from poems! I began to shout.
Poetry is like a sharp rock that you sit on and then you get up
and throw the rock into the water to get rid of it.
It can make you rock an invisible baby.
The moment to express it is the moment you have
… a lion sleeping in your mind and then bursting out to prey upon the paper.
Once you've sucked in you can never stop writing, but I did.
Each line is a different color sweeping across the page
Start with freshly ground vowels.
Can leave a big spot in your mind.
Plodding through an Open field, Everything Makes sense.
It's like riding an eclipse.

Afterword
Jonathan Skinner

Bird of Passage

Thinking of Jack now I see him up early, in bathrobe at the typescript and photocopy-laden desk in his Boulder office, amidst dictionaries, poetry books and field guides, musing over a yellow legal pad, Dot's Diner ballpoint in hand, or at the Selectric, typing up a letter to one of his many and various correspondents. Jack might be distracted by a squirrel's or sparrow's shenanigans out the window ("the squirrel in the Colorado blue spruce / is running wild"), or his attention might wander to Jennifer Heath's wild garden out back: "I fall to dream / in a field of Jenny."

These observations would make their way into Jack's letters: "Now it's the morning of 2012. What will fly away? Displace movement? Birdlist so far: robin (great monotone trill as I opened the front door), starling (faint squeal), then (from back door) English sparrow, crow songs."

In line with the "limitless variety" the world held for Jack, each day began a new list and ended with one or several poems. Jack's sense of nature always overstepped and upended categories. In another letter from San Francisco, he noted how he and Jenny enjoyed "the ontological endlessness of Cindy Sherman in one museum & quality dramatizations of nature in the science museum."

Jack's life and work perpetually activated such refreshing juxtapositions, including many insets of nature in the urban environment, as in his contribution to the *Avant Gardening* anthology, "A Few Crumbs from the Houston Street Median Stripe Naturewalk." Jack might have associated these "crumbs" and "stripes" with "spandrels," a term he borrowed from Stephen Jay Gould, for the ineradicable spaces left over from squaring an arch, to denote the "necessary fluff, the effluvia of a natural process." Jack's poetry "spandrelized" everything (nature, culture, language, corner pocket shots) through immersion and looking closely:

> Surrounded by bone, surrounded by cells, / by rings, by rings of hell, by hair, surrounded by / air-is-a-thing, surrounded by silhouette, by honey-wet bees, yet / by skeletons of trees, surrounded by actual, yes, for practical / purposes, people, surrounded by surreal / popcorn, surrounded by the reborn: Surrender in the center/ to surroundings.
>
> ("Ecology")

Jack was gifted with a lovely, expressive voice. I remember first hearing him sing passenger pigeon at Naropa University, as he read from "Passage," his great documentary ode to the extinct North American migrant, once so abundant its flight "darkened the sky / for three days": "Hoo woo!- oo-hoo, hoo, hoo."

I miss Jack's letters, but he has left us (with the help of numerous collaborators) a superabundance of carefully composed poetry, prose and genre-defying work. Jack's publishing affiliations remained largely small press local, with some forays into the Bay Area, New York or New England. Yet I am convinced that his work will find its place in our poetry canon beside the likes of Lyn Hejinian (with whom Jack collaborated extensively), Clark Coolidge or Ed Roberson.

I emphasize the work and the performances (for the latter, go online to hear Jack read "Recipe for a Blue Heron" and "Ecology," for the Poets' Co-op TV Show) because Jack may be best known for his prodigious teaching of poetry writing, over more than forty years to people of all ages, a proven pedagogy gathered in at least two volumes. An avid reader of science and aesthetic theory, Jack applied ideas from biology to his work in the schools, comparing visiting poets (with the "heirloom autonomy" of their strange DNA) to the "larger-than-life" mitochondria vital to the "cell life" of the classroom: "They're a bit weird but essential."

Jack also started teaching "Eco-Lit" at Naropa as early as 1989, before the academic discipline of ecocriticism had gotten off the ground and well before ecopoetics was a thing. Each year I received a stapled Eco-Lit anthology of his students' best writing. In this way, Jack's poetics have mutated out into the lives and work of literally thousands of poets. As someone who worked in factories for two decades (a toxic occupation that put Jack on oxygen in his latter years), with a decidedly non-elitist attention to creative spark, Jack was well aware of poetry's capacity to save lives.

Reading through a generous selection of Jack's poetry in *Red Car Goes By*, I note a shift right about the time (late eighties) that he started juxtaposing bird guide language with descriptions of factory life in his *Exchanges of Earth & Sky*. He moved from "I"-based descriptive narration to phenomenological observation. The "I" in Jack's later writing is decentered, "just a swirl," inviting in the collapse and ironies that "arbitrary connections" bring, flaunting literary taste with goofy catches of language and bodily frankness, bursting the bounds of "poem" and "voice" for a thornier (sometimes "pushy") process of thought.

The world pole / flips one more time, mechanically geo / mantric, shakes the pants off of objective dance to reveal gradual chance, just numbers having a ball, as the rationale of it all.

("Arguing with Something Plato Said")

Jack also wrote extended essays in verse, and vice versa, putting poetry into his prose. The delights of tongue-twisting words always came first. But from *Arguing with Something Plato Said* (1990) onwards—and evident in his sumptuous collaborations with Lyn Hejinian, their *Sunflower* (2000) being among my favorites—Jack's was serious play, with a philosophical bent, focused on the "extremes & balances" of a species whose passage is proving to be ephemeral yet catastrophic to its host planet: as Jack writes near the end of his passenger pigeon ode, "& we are / birds of passage"

Jack's "life's work" of this thought was put together as *Second Nature*, a book that, in Jack's own words, "ranges from more-or-less reasonable exposition through surprise-laden antisyntax, sweet field views, satire & protest, lists, found poems, rants, offbeat metrical sonnets, happenings in a universe of mice, concrete compositions, woodsy memoir, eco-theory, acrostics, misquotes, collaborations, recipes, interview excerpts and possibility-catalogs, finding humor (incongruity) in all corners." It's one of the most various, richly interlocking texts I know.

More than anything, I remember and miss Jack's humor—"We've got about two feet of snow all around us! We're lucky to have it & lucky it's two feet —it can get up and walk away." I recall Jack's high tenor laugh, or gawp of delight at a fun line in a "pass the poem" collaboration. Or the way he would often close his letters with a whimsical sign-off, "May all your camels sip Bacardi through silver straws." Or with a more educational salute, "May all your camels play guitar like Roy Smeck."

As I edited Jack's *Second Nature*, with Andrew Schelling, Marcella Durand, and Elizabeth Robinson, Jack noted heartily, at age eighty, "I AM STILL learning." I will be forever grateful to Jack not only for his writing, his bird-listing, and his advocacy for vulnerable small invertebrates, but for his spirit, for teaching us to keep learning, to never be bored, and to roll with contingency: "Yesterday's walk (Boulder Valley Ranch) yielded lark sparrows, a butter-breasted chat, a big redtail, kingbirds, & I'm outa paper."

—excerpted from "In Memoriam," *Poetry Project Newsletter*,
December 2017/January 2018

Jonathan Skinner has authored the poetry collections Chip Calls, Political Cactus Poems, Birds of Tifft *and* Warblers, *in addition to numerous critical essays, and is founding editor of* ecopoetics. *He teaches in the Writing Program and in the Department of English and Comparative Literary Studies at the University of Warwick.*

ACKNOWLEDGEMENTS

Jack Collom died before he could see his final manuscript published and before he could express his thanks to those who helped make publication possible. Much, huge gratitude goes to Swanee Astrid for her intrepid work toward contacting Spuyten Duyvil, and who helped Jack and me in so many other ways; to Lisa Birman for suggesting the press; to Anne Waldman, Lyn Hejinian, Merrill Gilfillan, Andrew Schelling and others for their encouragement and assurances that this is the right path; Spuyten Duyvil's patient, creative Aurelia Lavalle and T. Thilleman, who worked diligently to make *Partly* a volume Jack would, I know, be proud of.

My eternal gratitude goes to Rickie Solinger for her archival talents and unshakeable friendship that's held things together for me during the past year; Gerard Swartz, Jack's boyhood friend whose support helped move this project along; and Reed Bye for his unflagging comfort and assistance at all levels on all things perhaps most especially his meticulous attention to this manuscript. Knowing Jack and his poetry so well (a forty-plus-year friendship), Reed helped to shape this book as no one else could.

Thanks and love to Jack's children, Christopher, Nathaniel, Franz, and Sierra Collom; to my children, Matthew and Robin Heath, Sarah Bell-Springer and Scott Springer, as well as our three grandchildren, Josh, Cameron and Kate; and to Jack's sister, Jane Wodening. Thanks to Anne Becher; Ken Bernstein; Crystal Brakhage; Julie Carpenter; Susie Chandler; Nan DeGrove; Marcella Durand; Felicia Furman; Sam Fuqua; Dan and Susie Hankin; Ana María Hernando; Tim Z. Hernandez; Stefan Hyner; Elena Klaver; Laura Marshall; the Martinez family; E.J. McAdams; Joe Richey; Val Wheeler; Sherry Wiggins and Jamie Logan; Peter Lamborn Wilson; Andrew Wille; and the Word By Word writers. Thanks to Naropa University for hosting a fabulous, unprecedented memorial; to E.J. McAdams and Marcella Durand for hosting a splendid memorial bird walk and poetry reading in Central Park; to the Boulder Public Library for presenting a warm, joyful tribute to Jack's teaching; and many more too numerous to name in this limited space.

I thank the poets—Jack's comrades in verse—who provided the marvelous and heartfelt blurbs for this book. And many, many thanks to Margaret Ronda for her brilliant foreword and Jonathan Skinner for his beautiful afterword.

—JKH

Jack Collom (1931-2017) was a prolific poet, an adjunct professor and Outreach director of Naropa University's Jack Kerouac School of Disembodied Poetics, where, in 1989, he pioneered Eco-Lit, regarded as the first ecology literature course in the United States. His avid interest in science and nature informed much of his work, notably in the books *Blue Heron & IBC*, *What a Strange Way of Being Dead*, *Arguing with Something Plato Said*, *Red Car Goes By*, *Exchanges of Earth and Sky*, *The Task*, and *Second Nature*, which won the 2013 Colorado Book Award. His writings and essays about the environment were published in, among many others, *ecopoetics*, *The Alphabet of the Trees: A Guide to Writing Nature Poetry*, and *ISLE, the journal of the American Society for Literature and the Environment*. He was a devoted collaborator, publishing works with other poets such as Reed Bye, Elizabeth Robinson and Lyn Hejinian. In the mid-1970s he began teaching in poets-in-the-schools programs, a practice he continued for the rest of his life. Teachers and Writers Collaborative published his books about teaching: *Moving Windows: Evaluating the Poetry Children Write*, the influential *Poetry Everywhere: Teaching Poetry Writing in Schools and in the Community* (with Sheryl Noethe), and an edited volume, *A Slow Flash of Light: An Anthology of Poems about Poetry*. He was a great advocate for teaching poetry beyond the conventional classroom: in prisons, senior centers, halfway houses, wildlife refuges, and other unusual contexts. He read and taught throughout the United States, and in Latin America and Europe, and received numerous grants and awards, including two National Endowment for the Arts Poetry Fellowships and a fellowship from the Foundation for Contemporary Arts. One of his favorite children's poems was by a wise sixth-grader, who wrote: "In our wildest dreams/Our days are numbered."

www.ingramcontent.com/pod-product-compliance
Lightning Source LLC
Chambersburg PA
CBHW051246110526
44588CB00025B/2897
* 9 7 8 1 9 4 7 9 8 0 4 5 7 *